THE ALBERT SHAW LECTURES ON DIPLOMATIC HISTORY

Under the Auspices of the

WALTER HINES PAGE SCHOOL OF INTERNATIONAL RELATIONS

By the liberality of Albert Shaw, Ph. D., of New York City, The Johns Hopkins University has been enabled to provide an annual course of lectures on Diplomatic History. The Lectures, while continuing to be included in the regular work of the Department of History, have since the establishment of the Page School of International Relations, in 1930, been placed under its auspices.

ALBERT SHAW LECTURES ON
DIPLOMATIC HISTORY

1899. JOHN H. LATANÉ. The Diplomatic Relations of the United States and Spanish America. 1900. (Out of print.)

1900. JAMES MORTON CALLAHAN. The Diplomatic History of the Southern Confederacy. 1901. (Out of print.)

1906. JESSE SIDDALL REEVES. American Diplomacy under Tyler and Polk. 1907. $1.75.

1907. ELBERT JAY BENTON. International Law and Diplomacy of the Spanish-American War. 1908. $1.75.

1909. EPHRAIM DOUGLAS ADAMS. British Interests and Activities in Texas, 1838-1846. 1910. (Out of print.)

1911. CHARLES OSCAR PAULLIN. Diplomatic Negotiations of American Naval Officers, 1778-1883. 1912. $2.25.

1912. ISAAC J. COX. The West Florida Controversy, 1798-1813. 1918. $3.00.

1913. WILLIAM R. MANNING. Early Diplomatic Relations Between the United States and Mexico. 1916. $2.50.

1914. FRANK A. UPDYKE. The Diplomacy of the War of 1812. 1915. $2.75.

1916. PAYSON JACKSON TREAT. The Early Diplomatic Relations Between the United States and Japan, 1853-1865. 1917. $2.75.

1921. PERCY ALVIN MARTIN. Latin America and the War. 1925. $3.50.

1923. HENRY MERRITT WRISTON. Executive Agents in American Foreign Relations. 1929. $5.00.

1926. SAMUEL FLAGG BEMIS. Pinckney's Treaty: A Study of America's Advantage from Europe's Distress, 1783-1800. 1926. (Out of print.)

1927. BRUCE WILLIAMS. State Security and the League of Nations: A Survey of the Movement for State Security from the Treaty of Versailles to the Locarno Conference. 1927. $2.75.

1928. J. FRED RIPPY. Rivalry of the United States and Great Britain over Latin-America, 1808-1830. 1929. $2.75.

1931. CHARLES CALLAN TANSILL. The Purchase of the Danish West Indies. 1932. $3.50.

1932. DEXTER PERKINS. The Monroe Doctrine, 1826-67. 1933. $3.50.

1933. CHARLES SEYMOUR. American Diplomacy During the World War. 1934. $3.00.

1935. FRANK H. SIMONDS. American Foreign Policy in the Post-War Years. 1935. $2.00.

AMERICAN FOREIGN POLICY
IN THE
POST-WAR YEARS

LONDON: HUMPHREY MILFORD
OXFORD UNIVERSITY PRESS

THE ALBERT SHAW LECTURES ON DIPLOMATIC HISTORY, 1935

THE WALTER HINES PAGE SCHOOL OF INTERNATIONAL RELATIONS

American Foreign Policy

in the

Post-War Years

BY

FRANK H. SIMONDS, Litt. D.

BALTIMORE

THE JOHNS HOPKINS PRESS

1935

COMPOSED AND PRINTED IN THE UNITED STATES OF AMERICA
BY THE LORD BALTIMORE PRESS, BALTIMORE, MARYLAND

To

DR. ALBERT SHAW

Gratefully recalling twenty years of association
on the *Review of Reviews* which remain one
of the pleasantest memories of
my life as a journalist

PREFACE

In their original form the six chapters of this book constituted a series of lectures delivered at the Walter Hines Page School of International Relations at The Johns Hopkins University. They were made possible by the Albert Shaw Foundation. I have revised the lectures to take advantage of many valuable suggestions made in the discussions which followed my talks and for which I express my gratitude to my hearers. I desire also to acknowledge my indebtedness to Frederick S. Dunn, Executive Secretary of the School, for his unfailing help and courtesy. Finally, my thanks are due to my daughter, Mrs. Lovell Thompson, for invaluable editorial assistance.

F. H. S.

Blighty,
Snowville, N. H.
July, 1935.

CONTENTS

INTRODUCTION

The design of this book is to present a brief and critical review of American foreign policy in the post-war years. Necessarily such a review must deal extensively with the relation of the United States to the League of Nations and to the World Court, but only cursorily with these international institutions themselves. As far as American policy itself is concerned, so far the following chapters must suffice. In respect of the League and Court, however, a further discussion is, perhaps, required.

The case against the League, which is voiced by nationalists in all countries and urged with particular vehemence by American isolationists, is well known. It rests upon the assertion that the original conception of Wilson, his dream of peace assured by world cooperation, was an illusion and that the Geneva experiment is utterly Utopian. Furthermore, while to the European opponents of the League, it has seemed futile, to the American, it has appeared fraught with extreme peril to their own country.

There exists, however, another case against the League which is less familiar. Those who urge it—and to their camp the present author belongs —are neither nationalists nor isolationists. On the contrary, they believe in international cooperation recognizing it as a means to promote an understanding between peoples, which must reduce the number of conflicts even if it does not abolish war altogether. These critics of Geneva, therefore, not only accept the League in principle but American membership as well. They are convinced, nevertheless, that in their present form, both the League and the Court constitute obstacles not aids to international understanding.

This conviction is, moreover, based upon a rejection of the principle of coercion as applied to the problem of world peace through the League. Those who hold to this view believe that the attempt to require the League to employ coercion not merely explains its present failure but also, if persisted in, will insure its ultimate ruin. And it must be evident that, if this thesis can be sustained, the argument for American membership in League and Court alike must fall of its own weight.

At the outset of a discussion of this point of view, it is necessary to revert to the basic principle of the American democracy, which asserts that just governments derive their authority from the consent of the governed. It is self-evident that this principle must apply with equal force to an international institution designed to perform universally any portion of the tasks which fall to the lot of a national government. For, in both instances, without consent there must be tyranny.

There is a second American principle not less applicable. What Wilson undertook to do at Paris was to create a world state which, in part at least, should play the rôle in respect of the sovereign nations of the world which the federal government of the United States had long played vis-à-vis the sovereign states of the American Union. The federal government has, however, been able to play its rôle only because it had been invested with certain powers, delegated to it by the states, themselves. Such delegation, moreover, necessarily involved a sacrifice of sovereignty by the states. Nor was there any other source of power for the League than a similar delegation of power by the member nations. Consent and delegation were, then, the fundamental principles upon which any League or Court had to be established, if they were to repeat internationally the success of the American federal government nationally.

When, at Wilson's behest, the Paris conference had established a League of Nations by means of the peace treaties and invested it with a constitution, which was the Covenant, and, through the Covenant, bestowed upon it executive, legislative and judicial branches, which were the Council, the Assembly and the World Court, two things still remained to be done. First, the consent of all peoples had to be acquired for the new international institution. Second, the member nations had to determine what fraction of their sovereign rights they would delegate to the League.

It was, moreover, at this point that failure began. For by the same peace treaties which established the League there were imposed upon the defeated nations territorial changes, financial burdens and unilateral disarmament provisions which were inequitable and therefore intolerable. Because they were helpless, the vanquished countries were compelled to ratify these treaties but, from the start, they did not disguise their resolution to procure revision by peaceful means if possible but by force if necessary.

The League was thus charged with the task of administering and enforcing a system of treaty law which the German, Austrian, Hungarian, Bulgarian and Turkish peoples all refused to accept voluntarily. Under such circumstances, if the condition of consent were to be fulfilled, Geneva had to be endowed with the authority to revise or repeal such portions of the treaty law of the Paris settlement as were unjust. And the World Court had to be invested with the power to pronounce these laws invalid when they were manifestly contrary to public policy, which in this instance was international cooperation. These steps involved the delegation by the member nations to the League and Court of the power to revise existing treaty law in all respects.

Otherwise it must be clear that the League and Court would be condemned for the future to accept as immutable laws which were themselves indubitably unfair and unjust. And as long as it was without power to change these laws, so long the victims of these treaty statutes would withhold their consent from the League and the Court. They might formally enter both, hoping to obtain at Geneva and The Hague that relief to which they were entitled, but once they had become satisfied that such relief was not to be found, then they would see both the League and the Court as instruments to perpetuate injustice and not to preserve peace.

But the countries which were the beneficiaries of the peace treaties were utterly unwilling to invest the League or the Court with the authority to revise the treaty law, because such revision would inevitably require of them sacrifices in territory, indemnities or security. On the contrary, they sought to have the League invested with the physical force requisite to defeat any challenge to the treaty law. But this was impossible because the countries which had shared in the victory were not equally concerned with the perpetuation of the peace treaties.

Thus the United States, for example, having no interest whatever in the preservation of the territorial *status quo* of the Paris settlement and no substantial stake in the fulfilment of the repara-

2

tions provisions of the Treaty of Versailles, refused to share in the responsibilities for the enforcement of the peace treaties, which membership in the League would involve. In the same fashion, the British, although they joined the League, nevertheless reserved to themselves the right to decide when and where they would assume responsibility for the enforcement of treaty law. And, in practice, all other peoples followed the British example.

The League of Nations and the World Court were thus tied to that body of death which was the treaty law of Paris and were also deprived of any authority to revise that law, notorious as were certain of its injustices. They were also without the means necessary to enforce the treaty law which they could not amend. Actual enforcement, therefore, became the task of those countries directly interested in the perpetuation of this law. To fulfil that task, too, the interested countries made various military alliances, defensive in purpose but designed to prevent any change in treaty laws, which were themselves irreconcilable with any idea of justice.

In addition, the European states headed by France, which were interested in preserving the *status quo,* were able to establish for themselves a predominant position both in the League and in the Court. World Peace and the *status quo* of the Treaties of Versailles, St. Germain, the Trianon, Neuilly and Sèvres thus became identical concerns of the League and Court—although by war the Turks presently freed themselves from the restraints of the Treaty of Sèvres. Any nation seeking to challenge or evade the provisions of this body of treaty law could be haled to Geneva or The Hague and there tried by the Council or Court in both of which the influence of France and her allies was supreme. If, moreover, judgment were entered against the defendant, then the right of coercion would be vested with the beneficiaries of the existing treaty law.

Two illustrations will suffice to demonstrate the fashion in which this system operated. In his Fourteen Points, Wilson had proclaimed the principle of Self-Determination. In the armistice terms, the defeated nations had been promised that the Fourteen Points should be the bases of the later treaties of peace. Nevertheless, the Treaties of Versailles and St. Germain denied to the Germans and Austrians the right to unite, which they had claimed.

This denial, which was in fact a violation of the terms of the armistice, did not flow from any consideration of right or justice. On the contrary, it had its origin exclusively in the concern for their own security of the French, Italian and Czech peoples, for whom the union of the Austrians and Germans seemed the promise of a restoration of the *Mitteleuropa* of the war. When, therefore, eleven years later, the German and Austrian governments undertook to establish a customs union between the Reich and the Republic, France and her allies invoked the treaty law (which, in the meantime, had been reaffirmed in loan agreements Austria had been compelled to subscribe to) and carried their case to the World Court.

As in the original demand of the Austrians and Germans for a political *Anschluss,* so in this later attempt at customs union there was nothing unreasonable. It was not pretended by France and Italy that the action of the German and Austrian governments was contrary to the will of these two peoples. It was not argued that such a customs union was economically undesirable. Instead, the issue was narrowed to the question of whether this project was consistent with treaty law, restated in the debt contracts. And, on that issue, the World Court, through the votes of judges controlled by the French and their allies, pronounced the union illegal.

Precisely in the same fashion, when the Germans, after fifteen years of vain effort to obtain a revision of the military clauses of the Treaty of Versailles, finally quit both the Disarmament Conference and the League and presently announced their purpose to rearm in defiance of treaty law, appeal was again made to Geneva. Once more, too, no fair-minded person could fail to perceive the injustice of a law which compelled the great German nation to remain disarmed on an armed continent.

The law which Germany repudiated by her own action was in itself unjust and absurd. Nevertheless the Council of the League condemned the German action as illegal and threatened a resort to coercion if it were followed by any attempt by similarly unilateral action to revise the other provisions of treaty law which compelled Germany to keep her frontier provinces unfortified alike in the west and in the east.

This decision of the Council was rendered at the dictation of the French, British, Italian and Soviet representatives, that is, of statesmen whose views were determined not by any concern for the justice of Germany's claims but purely and simply by the fact that justice for Germany might involve insecurity for their own countries. Thus as the Court had been exploited in 1931, the League was employed in 1935 to sustain treaty law which was inconsistent with justice and had been imposed upon defeated peoples by the bayonets of their conquerors.

In Europe, then, the League could not—and cannot—do justice. It has become an instrument to perpetuate wrongs and is always available to the beneficiaries of such wrongs, which have been established in treaty law, but is never within the grasp of those who seek to escape from these inequalities. In Asia, however, the failure of the League has been of a different sort, for Japanese action in Manchuria constituted a patent violation of treaty law, which not only was just but, in addition, had been voluntarily accepted by the Japanese.

What Japan did had no justification other than that resting upon the claim that national necessities were above all treaty law, even when that law had been sealed by Japanese consent. In the face of Japanese aggression, China took her case to Geneva in accordance with the procedure laid down in League practice. In the name of justice and on the basis of a self-evident violation of treaty law, China asked the League to do as the World Court had done in the matter of the Austro-German Tariff Union, when it compelled the abandonment of the project.

But in the Manchurian Affair the League could do nothing for China because the member nations and, in practice, Britain, France and Italy, which alone possessed the means to act, did not see their own interest sufficiently compromised by Japanese aggression to warrant assuming the risks incident to any resort to coercion. They were willing to condemn aggression by words but beyond that they would not go. Yet, even in the face of this self-restraint on the part of the League, Japan left Geneva.

The Austrian, German and Chinese episodes must, therefore, demonstrate how inexact is the description of the League and the Court as constituting a collective system to insure world peace. On the contrary, they are effective instruments of countries which have selfish reasons for desiring the perpetuation of a *status quo* created by treaty law, whenever their own interests are directly engaged. Accordingly, not merely may the League and Court be invoked successfully to perpetuate injustice but both can also be summoned vainly to enforce just laws.

The two basic requirements of any successful national or international institution, namely, consent of the governed and delegation of powers by the member states, have, therefore, never been fulfilled by the League and Court. Not only have the defeated nations of the World War refused to accept the treaty law of the Paris settlement as just and, therefore, binding upon themselves but also the Japanese have declined to accept permanently the treaty law of the Washington Conference, to which they once subscribed willingly. In the same fashion, all member countries have refused to permit the League to revise treaty laws advantageous to themselves and declined to employ their forces to carry out League decisions, save when their interests would be served by coercion.

In effect, therefore, the League of Nations, like the Holy Alliance before it, constitutes an international institution which, in the name of world peace, is employed to perpetuate a *status quo* created by victory in war. Nominally universal, where Alexander's device was purely European,

Wilson's prescription has actually been restricted to similar limits. Described as a collective system, moreover, the League is actually nothing of the sort. On the contrary, it has become the means by which four great powers, similarly fearful of Germany, can clothe concern for their own security with the color of solicitude for world peace. But, in reality, the contemporary attitude of Britain, France, Italy and the Soviet Union toward Germany is identical with that of Great Britain, Austria, Prussia and Imperial Russia toward France after the Napoleonic wars.

Must the failure of the League be accepted as definitive, then, and the Geneva experiment abandoned? On the contrary, in its brief history the experiment has already demonstrated the value of an international organization which at once supplies a place and a machinery for international consultation. In both respects, it has constituted a gain for international understanding which is valuable beyond exaggeration. Outside of the field of controversial questions, too, no one longer questions its usefulness.

In so far as the League and the Court have failed, that failure has resulted exclusively from the attempt to invest them with responsibilities which could properly be assigned only to the agencies of a real superstate actually fulfilling the two essential conditions of consent and delegation. Nor is there any prospect that in any future which is calculable either condition will be fulfilled. For sovereign states are today equally unwilling to permit any international institution to modify their frontiers and to dictate the employment of their national forces to restrain aggression, where their interests are not directly at stake.

Under such circumstances, the whole idea of coercion is unsound. For the only form of coercion which is possible is that in which the League machinery is exploited by interested nations without regard to the moral aspects of the treaty law they invoke. It is true, also, that, although treaty law must always constitute legal warrant for any *status quo,* all previous efforts to perpetuate a *status quo* in the name of peace have failed, because they have been inconsistent with right and justice. Invariably the victors in war have sought to perpetuate the treaty law imposed upon their foes. Always they have called upon the vanquished to accept the new law as definitive. Habitually they have invited the neutrals to join in a so-called collective system to accomplish such an end.

But no *status quo* ever yet established in Europe after war has deserved to be perpetuated. Looking back upon the system of the Congress of Vienna, it is plain that, had it endured, it would have denied to most of the peoples of Europe, great and small, the right to independence and unity. Examining in the same fashion that *status quo* which the

wars between 1855 and 1877 had created in
Europe, and which Bismarck had sought to perpetuate by means of the Concert of Europe, it is
equally clear that inherent in it also were injustices
beyond palliation. Today, moreover, no one pre-
tends that the Paris settlement was free from
similar defects.

The flaw in most American thought about war
has resulted from the assumption that, because international conflict has become terrible beyond
exaggeration, it has also become criminal. Yet the
American Declaration of Independence asserted
the right of peoples to appeal to arms to escape
injustice. The identical right was, moreover, justly
and successfully asserted by most of the subject
or divided nationalities of Europe between 1815
and 1918.

Throughout history there have been just wars
and unjust wars and the problem of peace has always been the problem of finding a substitute for
war to remedy injustice and to defeat aggression.
American advocates of the League are accustomed
to urge that the time has come to replace the practice of violence by the reign of law. In reality the
problem is far less simple since, before the reign
of law can be assured, there must be established
laws which are just and machinery for revising
such laws when they become obsolete.

As long as treaty law is unjust, so long will the
victims of that law seek relief. Until the benefi-

ciaries of such unjust law are ready to delegate
to some international authority the right and the
duty to revise this law, the victims will continue
to find in war the single available means to escape
from oppression. Under such circumstances, not
only is it impossible to abolish war, but also it is
immoral to attempt to abolish it by the use of force
against the oppressed.

Wilson endeavored to escape from this dilemma
by fashioning his Fourteen Points and attempting
to make them the foundation of the settlement
of Paris. He failed, however, and his failure, since
it resulted in the creation of a new body of treaty
law patently unjust, made it inevitable that there
should be future wars unless some method other
than war could be discovered to remedy the defects of the Treaties of 1919. And so far no such
method has been discovered.

Along with the failure to find a substitute for
just wars has gone the parallel failure to find a
means to prevent wars of aggression. That, in its
turn, has been due to two circumstances. In the
first place, there is no standard of right and wrong
which passes current across national frontiers.
And, in the second place, there is no sense of responsibility for the prevention of aggression common to all peoples and sufficiently strong to lead
them to risk their lives and property in a united
effort to restrain an aggressor, when his crime

is perpetrated in remote regions where they have no direct concern.

It follows then, quite obviously, that the machinery of Geneva and The Hague are inconsistent with the realities of the contemporary world. These realities are, too, not to be mistaken. The League can prevent neither just, nor unjust wars since it can neither end oppression nor halt aggression. On the contrary, as recent events have demonstrated, each time it attempts to prevent war by invoking treaty law, its efforts are foredoomed to failure either because the law itself is unjust or because the nation which violates it refuses to acknowledge its inherent justice.

Once, however, the attempt is made to invoke coercion against a great power, then the consequences are evident. Thus the United States originally declined to join the League because it would not assume responsibility for sharing in coercive undertakings. Subsequently Japan and Germany left Geneva and Italy has repeatedly threatened to go, if her Ethiopian enterprise produced repercussions such as were caused by the Japanese adventure in Manchuria and the German action in the matter of armaments. But a collective system from which four of the seven great powers are either absent or dissenting is, in itself, a *reductio ad absurdum* of the whole conception of the League of Nations.

Nor is there anything to be said for the various proposals to substitute so-called "pacific sanctions" for military coercion to enforce treaty law. For, on the one hand, these can be invoked against action to abolish unjust law and, on the other, a blockade or a financial embargo can easily produce misery hardly less considerable than war. And the nation which suffers from such sanctions will be far more likely to resort to war than to submit to coercion. As for the restraints alleged to reside in world opinion, which served as the basis for the empty pretensions of the Kellogg Pact, Japanese, German and Italian actions in recent years have disclosed that such a world opinion does not yet exist effectively.

On the other hand, what actually exists in the contemporary world is a vast system of treaty law having its origin in past wars. By virtue of this treaty law the Earth's surface is unequally divided amongst the several nations and many nationalities are still denied the right of ethnic unity. In the past, similar treaty law has proved impermanent because the nationalities denied liberty and unity have resorted to war to establish that right. And, in the post-war period various European nationalities, large and small, have disclosed the resolution to follow in the pathway of the past, if no other road be opened to them.

In very recent times, too, great peoples who have found their economic circumstances incomparably less attractive than those of their neighbors and have identified this unequal division of the material resources of the world as unjust, have similarly turned to war as the sole means of escape from conditions which are difficult today and promise to become desperate tomorrow. For these peoples, too, treaty law appears intolerable and revision the price of their own national survival. Fascism, National Socialism and Japanese imperialism all constitute expressions of the same spirit, which in each instance has been accompanied by the glorification of force and by the preparation for war.

Obviously the League of Nations and the World Court are as little able to bring about a revision of treaty law to abolish economic disparities as to eliminate ethnic inequalities. Inescapably, their mission has become that of upholding treaty law in the interests of the beneficiaries of that law. This fundamental division of nations into those opposing and those favoring revision of treaty law, therefore, constitutes an impassable barrier to the existence of any collective system, for there can be no basis for common action for these two groups.

As a consequence, precisely to the degree that the League has become the agency of the champions of existing treaty law, it has become unacceptable to those who demand revision whether on ethnic or economic grounds. In the end, therefore, it is condemned to decline to the status of a " rump "

parliament, composed exclusively of those satisfied nations for whom the existing treaty law
is the guarantee of possession of unequal bene-
fits. And it is in that direction that Geneva has
been drifting ever since the Japanese withdrawal
in 1931.

The alternative is to make the League a center
of international consultation and cooperation and
to eliminate the idea of coercion which is reducing
it to a mere headquarters of nations resolved to
preserve unmodified that system of treaty law of
which they are the beneficiaries. As the past years
have demonstrated, nations are ready to go to
council and not infrequently to agree in council.
When, moreover, agreement has not been reached,
appeal to coercion has at once deprived the League
of prestige, because it has failed, and of member
nations, because it was attempted.

One thing the past fifteen years have amply
proven, and that is that there is no peaceful way
to impose peace. As for the proposal to make war
to prevent war, that is a project worthy of Bedlam
but hardly appropriate for Geneva. In the light of
the lessons of the recent past, therefore, the League
should be relieved of every duty which involves
resort to coercion and pronouncement of moral
judgment and the task of the Court should be restricted to rendering decision in issues voluntarily
submitted to it by all parties at odds.

Once the principle of coercion flies out of the window of the new Palace of the Nations, moreover, the United States should enter by the front door. For then no valid reason for its absence will survive.

CHAPTER ONE

THE ECONOMIC ASPECT

On July 1, 1914, that is, on the eve of the World War, the United States was a debtor nation and its economic policy was consistent with its material circumstances. This policy was twofold. On the one hand, the country maintained an export surplus, and, on the other, it employed a protective tariff. Such a policy was, moreover, not merely traditional with the United States but the invariable practice of nations still in the frontier stage of national life. For, at that point in their existence, all countries are naturally concerned alike with the development of their territory and the creation of a national industry.

The frontier stage is, however, necessarily temporary. Sooner or later every country must come of age economically. When it arrives at maturity, too, then it becomes subject to the first commandment of international trade which runs—"As ye sell, so must ye buy." During the earlier phase nations naturally borrow abroad to build their railways and to create their industries. To meet the interest charges upon these borrowings, they export more than they import. And the creditor states, if they are to be paid at all, must accept payment in this form, for the debtor has nothing else to offer.

When a country has completed the frontier stage, it enters a new phase. It no longer requires foreign capital to develop its national resources but the debts it has incurred in the past still remain to be paid. So long, moreover, as these continue unpaid, it will still be obliged to maintain an export surplus to service and to extinguish them. But it will have every incentive to rid itself of this indebtedness and thus to abolish the mortgage upon its own national estate.

At the moment when the World War broke out, the United States had come to the end of its frontier stage. It was no longer borrowing foreign capital. On the other hand, it had not yet reached the point where its annual export surplus sufficed to service its previous borrowings. Thus, between 1896 and 1914, the amount it owed the world on balance had risen from $2,000,000,000 to $3,000,-000,000 but against this increase was to be set an expansion in domestic gold stocks due to surplus imports, amounting to something less than $200,-000,000. In effect, then, the United States was paying the larger part of the interest it owed abroad by means of its export surplus. And the moment was already close at hand when it would not merely be able to pay all of the interest charges but also to begin to reduce the principal as well.

The war hastened the arrival of that day. In fact, it did far more, for it transformed the United States from a debtor to a creditor nation. Where, on balance, the American debt to the world in 1914 had been $3,000,000,000, in 1921 the world owed the United States $4,000,000,000, war debts aside. Since the American material circumstances had now been radically altered, its traditional policy was no longer consistent with its changed circumstances. For, if it were to collect what was owed it abroad, it could no longer maintain an export surplus or preserve the existing protective tariff.

The reason for this was simple. Since there is no international money, trade between countries resolves itself into a gigantic " swop " at evens. To be paid for what it exports annually a country must each year purchase from abroad goods, services and gold to an identical amount. It can, if it chooses, accept the notes of its customers for the difference between its own exports and imports and thus temporarily maintain an export surplus. But, in effect, this is merely postponement and it is steadily piling up abroad an accumulation of goods and services, which it must one day take back, if it is ever to be paid.

For convenience, foreign debts are measured in terms of money, but, in practice they represent goods, services and gold. Thus the $4,000,000,000 which the world owed the United States in 1920 apart from the war debts, represented the surplus of goods sold and services rendered abroad by America in the years between 1914 and 1920. To collect these debts, and to collect the interest due upon them annually, the United States had to take its payment in kind. And since, at the moment, the debtor states were holding on to their gold to support their currencies, payment had to be accepted in goods or services.

Before 1914, the countries which were America's creditors had, without exception, maintained an import surplus. Since, however, they had been unwilling to accept enough goods and services from the United States to meet the annual interest due them on past lendings to America, they had re-lent to the United States that part of the sums due for which they did not accept payment in goods and services. The United States was now bound to follow the same course. If, however, by insisting upon maintaining an export surplus, it refused to take any payment in kind and, in addition, further expanded the sum already owing it from abroad, by an annual excess in exports, then the amount due would mount steeply through the operation of compound interest until it attained unmanageable proportions.

That was what did actually happen. The United States refused to modify its traditional policy. As a result, between 1920 and 1930 its exports, goods, services and gold included, amounted to $66,500,-

000,000 and its imports to but $66,000,000,000 and the difference constituted an export surplus of $500,000,000. Merely through normal trade, therefore, $500,000,000 was added to the capital of its foreign loans. In the meantime nothing had been paid upon the principal and the annual interest charges were, therefore, pyramided upon the original obligation. Thus, had no other factor been involved, the world's debt to the United States must at least have doubled in the eleven years between 1920 and 1930.

But something else did happen. The United States resolved to collect the war debts, which were eventually to be capitalized at $12,000,000,000. Annual payments upon these were, moreover, to start at $250,000,000, rise shortly to $450,000,000 and remain at that peak level for upwards of half a century. But how was this further payment to be accepted? It, too, could be made only in goods, commodities and gold, and the gold supplies of the debtor countries were inadequate to meet any considerable fraction of their debts.

The accidents of war, together with the decision to collect the war debts had thrust the United States into the position of a creditor country upon a grand scale. On balance, the world now owed it $14,000,000,000, whereas in 1914 it had owed the world $3,000,000,000. Only one country had ever occupied a similar position and that was Great Britain. It had, moreover, taken the British the

better part of a century to build up a foreign holding of $20,000,000,000 and the United States had
acquired a foreign investment three-quarters as
large in seven brief years.

If the American people were resolved to play
the part of a creditor country, which had been the
familiar rôle of the British for so long, then they
were also bound to adopt the British technique,
for none other was discoverable. Other countries,
too, notably France and Holland—and in the immediate pre-war years, Germany, as well—had, in
their turn, adopted the same technique with a
measure of success.

The smallest examination of the British system,
however, disclosed the significant fact that Great
Britain had prepared the way for its later performance as a creditor country by a major surgical
operation. By the repeal of the Corn Laws in 1846,
England had sacrificed its agriculture. Thenceforth it could export the production of its factories
and accept payment therefor in the form of foodstuffs and raw materials. Thus, before it became
a creditor country, it had, by adopting free trade,
opened its market to future debtors.

Since, after 1846, Britain's competitors continued to cling to their agriculture, British industry
long enjoyed a threefold advantage. Having ex-
perienced the Industrial Revolution first, it had
got the jump upon its competitors technically.
Thanks to free trade, it enjoyed cheap food and

thus comparatively low costs of production. Finally, since it exported goods and imported foods and raw materials, its ships were assured of a full cargo coming and going.

In fact, so great were British advantages, that in no long time it became evident that the domestic factories could produce more goods which foreign markets could absorb than the British market could accept payment for in raw materials and foodstuffs. As a consequence, England began, perforce, to lend her customers the difference. In that way she laid the foundations for her later position as the greatest creditor country on the planet.

But in making these loans the British did not, at least for many years, finance their industrial rivals but merely aided in the development of their agrarian customers. Up to the War, too, the British continued to accept at least a part of the interest due them annually in the form of goods and raw materials. The threefold basis of their technique was, therefore, the sacrifice of domestic agriculture to industry, the adherence to free trade and, finally, the constant re-lending abroad of that part of the interest upon foreign holdings for which they could not accept payment in kind.

Today it is possible to question whether, in the longer view, the British course in 1846 and the succeeding years was economically sound or socially wise. That it resulted in periodic financial losses of vast proportion is certain. That it produced social conditions which were undesirable is at least arguable. In the end, the war disclosed the extent to which Britain had become vulnerable through the decline of its agriculture, and in the post-war years, the policy of free trade broke down altogether and had to be abandoned. But what is not to be challenged, is the fact that the British method of playing the game of the creditor country was the single method possible and, if the United States were resolved to play that game, it was bound after 1920 to adopt the British technique.

In reality, however, that way was open to the United States only in theory and not in practice. No administration, whether Democratic or Republican, could even dream of following the British example of 1846 and scrapping American agriculture in order to expand foreign trade or to collect foreign debts. Not less absurd was the notion of reversing the process and sacrificing the factory while clinging to the farm. Actually, even before the war, the United States had become a country of a balanced economy. It had acquired a degree of economic self-sufficiency unapproached by any other nation. Between 1920 and 1930, moreover, a state of approximate balance existed between its imports and exports as in fact it had existed between 1896 and 1914. For, in the later years the excess of exports over imports, goods, services and gold included, was but $500,000,000.

When, however, the Harding administration, Congress and public opinion demanded first, that the war debts be collected, second, that the existing tariff schedules be not merely maintained but presently raised and, finally, when the private investors in foreign securities clamored for the payment of interest upon their investments, what could be done? Only one thing: the American investor, by still further purchases of foreign paper could supply the foreign debtors, governmental and private, with the means to meet the costs of their debts to the United States annually and to liquidate the costs of the American export surplus as well. If the United States refused to accept payment in goods and services, then, since the debtors lacked adequate gold reserves, Uncle Sam had to lend from one pocket what he presently put back into another.

Such was the process which was begun in 1921 and continued until 1930. Concerning these years, too, there has grown up a legend that the United States annually loaned abroad vast sums to finance its export surpluses and therefore, in effect, gave away its goods. In fact, however, during these eleven years there was a difference of but $500,-000,000 between what the United States sold and what it bought in goods, services and gold and this disparity in a total export trade of $66,500,000,000 was relatively insignificant, amounting to materially less than one-tenth of one per cent.

What actually occurred was that between 1920 and 1930 the interest charges upon the $14,000,-000,000 owed us from abroad, $10,000,000,000 in war debts and $4,000,000,000 in private investments, aggregated approximately $6,500,000,-000, while the total export surplus was $500,000,-000. The world, therefore, owed us $7,000,000,000 which it could not pay in gold, because it lacked the necessary amounts above what it needed to retain to protect its currency. The United States, on its part, refused to accept payment in goods or services. The deadlock was broken, however, by American citizens who invested $7,000,000,000 in foreign securities. And out of the proceeds of these purchases, foreign countries and corporations remitted the annual instalments due for goods, war debts and private investments.

Taken as a whole, the United States did not invest any fresh money in Europe in these years. But one group of American citizens paid the interest due to the American Treasury upon war debts and to another group of citizens upon their private investments and accepted foreign securities in return. When the crash ultimately came, as it was bound to come, the first group still held the $7,000,000,000 of foreign securities and the total debt of the world to the United States had expanded from $14,000,000,000 to $21,000,000,000 and was still increasing at the rate of more than $1,000,000,000 annually.

The fashion in which the war debts were " paid " in the post-war period was, moreover, identical with that in which they had been incurred. The United States did not send money abroad. On the contrary, it sent cotton and copper, petroleum and meats, steel and munitions. For these it took the notes of foreign countries. At the same time it borrowed from its own citizens by means of the Liberty Loans the money necessary to pay the domestic producers who had shipped these commodities abroad. The single real difference was that in the case of the $10,000,-000,000 of war debts the United States Treasury took the notes of foreign governments, while in that of the post-war loans it was the private investor who took foreign securities.

This performance endured for eleven years, that is, until the boom and crash in Wall Street at the close of 1929 ended the purchase of foreign securities by the American investor. When that operation ceased, then the game was up. But the wheels did not stop automatically, they simply slowed down progressively. By June, 1931, however, Germany was no longer able to go on with reparations payments and was in the throes of a banking crisis. The Reich was, moreover, unable to continue reparations payments because it had obtained the means to make these payments to the Allies by selling German securities in the United States. As for the Allies, they had passed German payments on to the United States on account of war debts.

When the banking crisis arrived in Germany, however, the United States investors had several billions of German securities in their possession and, if German finance collapsed, their losses were bound to be great. To save these investments, therefore, Mr. Hoover intervened with his Moratorium. By the terms of that proposal, the United States was to cease collecting the war debts for a year, and during the same period, the Allies, who were also the war debtors, were to stop exacting reparations payments from Germany.

The proposal was logical, because when the American investor stopped buying German securities, the Reich was without means to meet reparations. But it failed to save American investments, because Germany had still to meet the interest charges upon these. And, in the meantime, in order to protect the American market from foreign goods, German and otherwise, the Hoover administration had resorted to the Hawley-Smoot Tariff Law. Not being able to pay in goods, therefore, the Germans could only pay in so-called " blocked marks " negotiable only when expended for German goods and, therefore, of relatively small value to American investors, who could not profitably bring these goods home because of the domestic tariff barriers.

Meantime the economic blizzard had also hit England and, under its stress, the traditional policy of free trade had broken down. As a consequence of the French devaluation of the franc, of the German resort to "dumping" in a frantic effort to save the mark from a new inflation, and of the war debt payments to the United States, Great Britain was now " in the red." Thus the sum of British receipts for exports and interest upon foreign investments no longer sufficed to pay the costs of a vast import surplus together with the American debt instalments. In the face of this situation, therefore, Great Britain abandoned free trade and adopted a protective tariff, alike upon industrial and agrarian imports, thus revising her economic policy to conform with her new material circumstances.

In theory, England was now in the same situation as the United States, since both were creditor countries and both were also employing tariffs to protect the domestic market. In practice, however, the situations of the two countries were fundamentally different. For while the United States was approximately self-sufficient alike in industry and agriculture, Great Britain still remained, after 1931 as before, dependent upon the outside world for the bulk of its foodstuffs and raw materials, which, in the main, were supplied or could be supplied by her debtors. And, to facilitate this process of payment, the British manipulated their tariff to give a preferential position in their home market to their debtors, chiefly to the Dominions and the Argentine.

The adoption of a protective tariff by the British, unlike the passage of the Hawley-Smoot Tariff Bill by the American Congress, still left debtor countries with an opportunity to meet their obligations in the single fashion which was open to them, namely, by shipping commodities to the creditor country. And that was the inner significance of the Ottawa and Buenos Aires Agreements, which attracted anguished notice on the part of the American business world. Thus, even in the face of the great depression, the British continued to play the game of the creditor country according to the rules and to collect the bulk of their foreign debts. Losses they did suffer: but though large in themselves, they were slight by comparison with the American.

In December, 1932, moreover, the United States was confronted by a fresh crisis. The Hoover Moratorium had been designed to last but a year. It had been conceived as a temporary device to meet a transient emergency. But the emergency still endured and the old question of the war debts was up again.

Two possibilities there were, and only two: the debts might now be cancelled or the Moratorium prolonged. American public opinion was, however, still adamant against cancellation and, since the Moratorium had failed to save American in-

vestments in Germany, it had now become un-
popular. The survival of the delusion that Europe
could be made to pay, moreover, still obsessed a
people plunged into the depths of the greatest
economic crisis in their history. Struggling to meet
their own domestic debts, the people of the United
States viewed with indignation all proposals which
envisaged forgiving the foreigner his obligations
and shifting the burden of these to American
shoulders.

In the autumn of 1932, before the Hoover Moratorium had expired, the European states to which
Germany was bound to make reparations payments had at last faced the reality of the transfer
problem. They had set out originally to collect
vast sums from the Reich but, save in minor details they, like the United States in the matter of
the war debts, had been unwilling to accept payment in goods and services which were necessarily
competitive with their own. So long as the United
States investor had continued to lend to Germany,
her creditors had been able to take the proceeds
of these loans on account of reparations, but, when
the American source dried up, it became for these
countries a question of accepting goods and services or getting no reparations. And, so, at a conference in Lausanne, the Allied creditors of Germany had in fact cancelled reparations although
in form that cancellation was made contingent

upon similar American action in respect of the war debts.

When, however, the United States not merely refused to cancel the war debts but also declined to prolong the Hoover Moratorium, France and Belgium defaulted at once, while Great Britain and Italy, after paying one more semi-annual instalment in full, resorted to the expedient of a " token payment." In the following year, too, when Congress passed and the President signed the Johnson Bill putting in the same category those countries which had defaulted outright and those which had resorted to the expedient of " token payments," Britain and Italy followed the example of France and Belgium and the tragi-comedy of " collecting " the war debts had its final curtain. For all practical purposes, the war debts were now dead, although it still remained possible that at some future time the debtor countries might remove the stigma of default by one final " token payment."

Nor was a considerable portion of the private investments, which in 1930 had amounted to $10,-000,000,000 in excess of foreign holdings of American securities, in much better stead. By April, 1935, this excess had shrunk to $6,000,000,000 in face value, and, in addition, the devaluation of the American dollar had further reduced the gold value of these securities by 41%. At best, therefore, the United States was now back about where it had started in 1921, when the surplus of its foreign holdings over alien investments in American securities had totalled $4,000,000,000.

In 1935, as in 1921, the United States still had an export surplus and was still collecting interest upon a portion of its foreign investments. But by that time a new expedient was being employed to evade the transfer issue, which, in fact, constituted the economic law of gravitation. Between 1921 and 1930, the illusion of debt collection had been kept alive by American purchase of foreign securities. Now it was being fostered by foreign payments in gold. Thus in 1934 the surplus of gold imports over exports of the United States was $1,250,000,000 in round figures and for the first quarter of 1935 it was $350,000,000. As the annual production of gold in the world is barely $1,000,000,000, the United States was, therefore, draining off the gold reserves of other countries and by this time had accumulated nearly 40% of the world's supply as against 7% held by Great Britain.

By no means all of this yellow flood represented interest payments or was due to an export surplus although these explained a substantial portion. In addition, foreign investors were buying back American holdings in the securities of their own countries at bargain prices and Americans who had transferred their resources abroad before the gold embargo were putting them back into American

stocks and bonds. The $8,000,000,00 in gold
which had now piled up in the American Treasury
vaults was, however, without practical value, beyond the part actually required for currency back-
ing, when and if stabilization presently came. For
it could only be used to purchase foreign goods
and commodities and against these, the Hawley-
Smoot Tariff Law still barred the door. Nor were
there wanting warning voices forecasting that this
enormous accumulation of gold could one day
serve as the basis for a credit inflation more ex-
tensive and ultimately more disastrous than that
of 1929.

Measured by any standard, therefore, it is plain
that the domestic consequences of the World War,
in so far as they transformed the Unites States from
a debtor to a creditor country, were catastrophic
and the attempt to collect the war debts was as futile as it was foolish. Nature, herself, by endowing
America with the riches of agriculture as well as
the resources of industry, had made it forever impossible for the United States to play the rôle of
a creditor country on the British scale. At most it
could only purchase abroad enough to enable it
to dispose of its own surplus in those goods and
commodities for the sale of which it must depend
upon the foreign market.

Since the United States, like all other countries,
was subject to the inexorable law that a nation can
sell only as it buys or, more exactly, that the sum

of what it collects on all foreign accounts must be balanced by what it pays abroad, it could only collect foreign debts if it reduced its domestic exports. The alternative was to pyramid the interest payments upon its foreign holdings, annually re-investing abroad the total of such payments. And that, of course, was what it did. But inevitably the structure thus erected by the operation of compound interest collapsed, once the American investor had declined to continue to leave his interest abroad.

In the United States the politician and the public man saw plainly that the foreign debts were just debts. They perceived with even greater clarity that if the alien debtor were forgiven them the domestic taxpayer would be compelled to shoulder the burden. But, at this point, both confused economics with ethics and concluded that what was theirs by right could be physically put in their possession. What remained hidden from them always was the fundamental truth that, at best, the costs of collecting the debts would equal the price of cancellation. For, to be paid, the United States had to accept annually goods and services to the value of the debt instalments and, in practice, this meant letting American workmen stand idle while foreign laborers performed their tasks.

The chapter in American History devoted to the effort to collect the credits, public and private, accumulated abroad by the United States as a consequence of the World War must, therefore, constitute the record of a vain attempt to ride two horses at once, an attempt that resulted, as was inevitable, in a fall between the two steeds. Between 1921 and 1935, four administrations with equal enthusiasm and energy endeavored to discover some method by which the people of the United States could simultaneously enjoy the privileges which belong to a debtor nation and harvest the profits which fall to the share of a creditor country. But, since the two things are mutually exclusive, the result of a decade and a half of striving was disillusionment abroad and disaster at home.

Nor were the contradictions in American economic policy in the post-war years confined to the foreign debts; on the contrary, they were disclosed in at least two other important fields. Of these, the first was that of currency stabilization and the second that of silver. To the London Economic Conference in 1933, the President sent a delegation headed by the Secretary of State and instructed to share in a world wide effort to bring about the stabilization of currencies. And its instructions had been formulated after Mr. Roosevelt had engaged in personal conversation with J. Ramsay MacDonald, the Prime Minister of Great Britain, and Edouard Herriot, former premier and special representative of France.

Hardly had the Conference convened, however, when the reports of approaching agreement upon a program of stabilization produced a sudden fall in prices in the United States. That fall was inevitable because at the moment the Roosevelt administration was seeking to raise domestic prices by currency manipulation and world stabilization would necessarily end this experiment. In effect, therefore, while the President was undertaking to promote currency stabilization in London he was preventing it at home.

Confronted by the domestic repercussions of his foreign undertaking, moreover, Mr. Roosevelt suddenly and brusquely intervened at London, directed the American delegation to reverse their course and called upon the representatives of other countries to lay aside the projected stabilization, the major objective of the Conference, itself, and address themselves to other tasks. As a result, the Conference collapsed ignominiously and the statesmen of the world were left bewildered and indignant at the spectacle of a great nation which had visibly attempted to travel in opposite directions at the same moment. Yet, from first to last, it should have been evident to the dullest mind that it was just as little possible to combine the two projects of stabilization abroad and progressive devaluation at home as it was to play the rôles of debtor and creditor countries simultaneously.

As to the question of silver, in the Manchurian Affair the Hoover administration had taken an uncompromising stand in support of China and thus in opposition to Japanese action, which constituted a violation of the Covenant of the League of Nations, the Kellogg Pact and the Washington Treaties. It had firmly refused to recognize Manchukuo. It had publicly proclaimed the Stimson Doctrine, permanently denying American recognition of all territorial changes brought about by acts of violence. It had even associated itself with the League of Nations in rebuking Japan by means of the Lytton Report, in the making of which an American representative had shared.

American action had been dictated by two things, the country's traditional policy of the Open Door in China and its natural desire to see the sanctity of international agreements preserved. Materially we were interested because of the former consideration, morally we were concerned because of the latter. And while the United States had refrained from taking up arms to prevent an invasion of Chinese sovereignty, it had spared no other effort on behalf of a country patently the victim of an act of deliberate aggression.

The Hoover administration had thus made it clear that Chinese independence was a concern of American policy. Nor did the Roosevelt administration, when it came to power, repudiate that policy, since it continued to deny recognition to Manchukuo. Nevertheless, in 1934, when Congress passed the Silver Purchase Bill, the President signed it. The effect of this enactment upon the domestic economic conditions of China was catastrophic and the result was, therefore, to drive the Chinese, willy-nilly, into the arms of Japan. Thus while, on the one hand, the United States had risked a war with Japan on behalf of Chinese independence, on the other, it had contributed incalculably to insuring Japanese domination over China.

Alike in the matter of the war debts, of currency stabilization and of China, the United States in the post-war period had been called upon to make a clear decision. In all three instances, it had to do one of two things. In all three, however, it deliberately undertook to do both things at once and the results were similarly if not equally disastrous. On each occasion, too, an American administration approached its problem without any clear perception of the principles involved or the issues at stake. Without exception, also, when decision was actually made, it was dictated exclusively by concern for domestic political conditions and without thought for the material consequences alike national and international.

In sum, throughout the post-war years the objective of American foreign policy in its economic

detail was to fit the new material circumstances
of the United States to pre-war pattern. But, since
these new circumstances could not thus be assimi-
lated, the results of the attempt were always chaotic
and not infrequently catastrophic.

Chapter Two

WORLD PEACE

Before the World War, American activity on behalf of international peace was slight. To be sure, the United States was represented at the two futile congresses held at The Hague and even at the Algeçiras Conference, where the achievement was still less impressive than at the Dutch capital. On the whole, however, the government and people of the United States viewed the possibility of war in Europe with much the same detachment which they would have displayed toward disturbances on another planet.

The World War, however, brought about a change in the American point of view. The fact that the United States had been dragged into a European war and had therein sacrificed lives and expended treasure with no other profit than the empty vindication of its maritime rights brought the fact home to the American people that they had a vital interest in preventing another war in the Old World. In addition, in the post-war period, the war debts and private investments together constituted a material stake in Europe certain to be affected adversely by another conflict.

European peace, therefore, was recognized on all sides as a legitimate concern of American foreign policy. Two questions, however, were thus raised immediately, for to promote peace as to wage war, it is necessary not merely to decide upon methods but also to provide means. And, in practice, at a certain point, the two processes may easily merge. How, then, was the United States to promote world peace and how far was it willing to engage its material and military resources in the task?

Both questions were still unanswered when the Republican Party returned to power on March 4, 1921, but its previous performances had visibly restricted its future freedom of action. At Paris, Mr. Wilson, by his Peace Treaties, which had established the League of Nations, had made a definite response to both questions. The task of preventing war was for the future to be transferred to the new international institution which was to be established in Geneva and the military and financial resources of all the member countries were to be pooled in the collective effort to end international conflict. In effect, a world partnership in peace had thus been created and the Democratic President had envisaged America's full participation in this partnership. This plan had, moreover, envisaged the assumption by the United States of an equal share in the responsibilities of the common undertaking.

In 1919, however, the United States had rejected Mr. Wilson's program and thus closed the road to Geneva. In the presidential election of 1920, too, the Republican Party had made the League the major issue of the contest. Woodrow Wilson, on his part, had accepted the challenge and described the election itself as " a solemn referendum." The result of this referendum, however, had been a decisive victory for the Republican opponents of American membership in the League and the Chief Magistrate, whom they then elected, came to the White House committed in advance to oppose any further attempt to lead his country to Geneva.

In theory, however, the American people had not, by their votes in 1920, renounced all concern for world peace. On the contrary, they had merely rejected the Wilsonian prescription. After, as before the election of Harding, material considerations, and moral as well, dictated that the United States should play its part in preventing a repetition of the events of 1914-1918. But how was it to fill this rôle, now that the League solution was out of the question? The problem was complicated, too, by certain ominous signs and portents in Europe.

In fact, although Germany under duress had accepted the Treaty of Versailles, it had found the terms intolerable. Already, therefore, it was plain that the German people would never endure the conditions of the Paris settlement beyond the moment when they had escaped from the exhaustion of the war and evaded the unilateral disarmament provisions of the Treaty itself. The resolution to challenge the Treaty of Versailles already existed, the moment when the challenge would be delivered was alone in doubt.

But to challenge the settlement of Paris was to precipitate a new conflict. For France and her associates, for whom treaty revision not only involved an immediate lessening of security but also, not impossibly, foreshadowed an eventual loss of territory, were prepared to resort to force rather than permit revision, as the French action in occupying the Ruhr presently demonstrated. These states, too, argued from the outset that there was no other way to preserve peace save to perpetuate the association of countries which had won the war. By that means, a combination of forces would be created beyond the capacity of Germany to challenge at the moment or in any time then calculable.

Great Britain, for her part, supported in principle by some of the neutrals of the war, urged that the true solution of the problem of peace was the revision of the Treaty of Versailles. Only if Germany were thus placated could the British discover any promise of real peace. But the British program at once encountered the uncompromising opposition of France and her allies. And Great Britain, herself, unaided by the United States, was

wholly unable to impose her solution of the problem upon France and the French allies. Either to
accept the French proposal, which involved the
permanent coercion of Germany or to support the
British project, which necessitated the immediate
coercion of the French must, moreover, involve the
Harding administration and the United States in
the European mess.

But the Harding administration was already
committed to a program of " Normalcy " which,
in the field of foreign policy, meant the avoidance
of foreign entanglements and the American people had, in 1920, backed that program by a decisive majority at the polls. Having rejected the
Wilson program, what had the Republican Party
now to offer in its stead? In practice, nothing, and
the French invasion of the Ruhr in January, 1923,
following shortly after an appeal to Paris to stay
its hand, made by Mr. Hughes, the American
Secretary of State, disclosed the impotence of the
Harding administration. In that speech made at
New Haven, Mr. Hughes had, however, dropped
a hint to Europe, which was later to be taken up
with enormous consequences for his own country.

In advance of the occupation of the Ruhr, the
Harding administration had, moreover, made an
ambitious attempt to combine moral concern for
peace with political isolation from European entanglements. Thus, during the Washington Naval
Conference of the winter of 1921-1922, the Presi-

dent had signed—and the Senate had later ratified
—those Treaties of Washington which not merely
bound all the signatory powers to respect the
status quo in the Far East and thus to maintain
the Open Door in China, but also to come to conference, in case of violation of these pacts by any
nation. Attached to that agreement, however,
there were no sanctions. America's hand were,
therefore, still free and the United States could decide as it chose when emergency arose.

Implicit in the Washington Treaties was the
idea of peace assured by self-denying ordinances.
All nations were to sign a pledge not to resort
to violence and such an act was, in itself, calculated automatically to close the door to future
aggression. If, however, contrary to all reasonable
expectation, some country broke its pledge, then
the signatory powers would come to conference
and back of them would be mobilized the overwhelming force of world opinion, which would
constitute an all-sufficing sanction, against which
no single nation would dare stand. The objective
of this device was to serve the cause of peace but
the method employed was designed to evade all
responsibility for maintaining it.

From Asiatic issues, the attention of the Harding administration was soon recalled to European
events. Despite Mr. Hughes's New Haven speech
the French had occupied the Ruhr. As for the Germans, when they had tried passive resistance the

result for them had been a worse disaster than the war itself. For inflation, employed in the vain hope of sustaining passive resistance pending expected Anglo-Saxon intervention, had completed the ruin of the middle class, without preventing eventual surrender to France. By September, 1923, therefore, Germany was forced to make a second armistice not less humiliating than that of November, 1918.

Victorious France had, however, collected no reparations and the French people were now tired of the Poincaré method and ready to listen to the counsels of moderation coming alike from London and Washington. Twice defeated, Germany was, also, brought face to face with the fact that any further attempt to challenge the Treaty of Versailles in present time was doomed to swift and costly failure. At this point then, the moment had come to take up the suggestion of Mr. Hughes's New Haven speech which was that Europe call in New World finance to redress the balance of the statesmanship of the Old.

Such was the prelude to the Dawes Plan which was actually made in London in 1924 and temporarily took the politics out of reparations and substituted American loans for French bayonets. Officially the United States was not represented in London. Like Cæsar's wife the Republican administration held itself above suspicion. But the American financiers were there and, subsequently, American loans in ever increasing volume were adventured in Europe. Contrary to the words of the Scripture, the United States was now attempting to establish its treasure on one continent and to keep its heart on another.

With the making of the Dawes Plan, following as it did the ratification of the Washington Treaties, there ensued a pause. In Europe the sun of Locarno soon shone brightly. At Geneva, Briand, Stresemann and Chamberlain, the great triumvirate of peace, treated Europe to a brief but brilliant period of tranquillity. Meantime, American loans were flowing into Europe, but, while our investment expanded, our isolation, so it was argued in America, still remained unimpaired.

By 1928, moreover, the American fear of the League of Nations and the concomitant dread of foreign involvement had somewhat died down. Europe now seemed peaceful and the moment was deemed propitious to take a forward step in the matter of world peace. Even then there was no disposition to join the League of Nations. On the contrary, by this time the Democratic party had accepted the decision of 1920 as final. Wilson's Covenant seemed as impossible as ever from the American point of view. Nevertheless, in view of the American material stake in Europe, cooperation with the League was at last judged to be as useful as it seemed safe.

A basis of cooperation, too, was discovered in the principle laid down in the Washington Treaties. In these, all the signatory nations had solemnly renounced any right or purpose to disturb the *status quo* in Asia, and thus to interfere with the Open Door in China. What could be more natural than to extend this self-denying ordinance to war, itself? If all nations, great and small alike, should now and forever renounce the employment of war as an instrument of policy, then war would be outlawed and, in addition, a bridge would thereafter exist between Washington and Geneva.

A bridge would exist because the nations which signed the new engagement, later to be known in America as the Kellogg Pact and in Europe as the Pact of Paris, were all, save the United States, members of the League. Accordingly, a country which violated the Covenant would similarly break its word pledged in the Pact, and, on the basis of this later breach of contract, the United States would have a warrant to consult with the League powers. In principle, therefore, although the Pact of Paris did not state the fact explicitly, the United States would thus be committed to consult, not merely with Asiatic powers, if the Treaty of Washington were broken, but also with European governments, if the Pact of Paris were breached on either continent.

5

But beyond consultation the United States was still not committed. Of course, it was not clear what practical good would result, if a country attended, resolved in advance to do nothing but talk. But that issue was not raised on this side of the Atlantic because at the time the convenient assumption that moral and not physical sanctions were the true solution of the problem had found general American acceptance.

The Kellogg Pact was, then, the high water mark of American endeavors for world peace which consisted in undertaking to combine the idea of political and military isolation with that of moral and material involvement. Neither on the Vistula nor on the Amur were we committed to any contract which might compel us to send our boys to fight abroad again. We were not bound to share in any military campaign to prevent aggression but only to serve on a jury which would pronounce judgment. And that judgment must prove effective, it was assumed, because behind it would stand the aroused conscience of mankind.

Enjoyment of the profits of world peace without payment of any of the expenses of international police force was thus in theory assured to the United States. But now that war had been outlawed as an instrument of policy what could be more appropriate than to support a program of disarmament in the world? What could be more advantageous for American interests, too, since a

Europe which owed us billions already and was
daily swelling that total was visibly hard put to it
to meet the twofold costs of debts and armaments? Perhaps we had not quite made the world
safe for democracy in 1919, but in 1932 there
seemed to be a chance to make it secure alike for
our ideals and for our investments.

Unhappily, however, before Europe could get
round to disarmament, disaster overtook it. By
1930 the Truce of Locarno had ended. Stresemann was dead, Hitler was just coming to the fore
in Germany and to forestall him the Republican
Cabinet undertook to bring about Austro-German
union by means of a common tariff. But this apparent effort to evade the Treaty of Versailles,
which had forbidden the *Anschluss,* brought
France, Italy and the Little Entente into action and
by April all Europe was in an uproar, that Europe,
to which American investors had by 1931 loaned
many billions lightheartedly.

Political strife, moreover, produced economic
and financial prostration. The collapse of the
Kreditanstalt in Vienna was the prelude to a bank
crisis in Berlin. Catastrophe in Germany was just
round the corner when the American holders of
German securities turned in despair to the Hoover
administration. If Germany collapsed economically and financially, then their billions were gone
irrevocably. In a word, although the American
administration was still happy in its political iso-

lation, innumerable American citizens were now in agony over their pecuniary involvement.

Accordingly, Mr. Hoover proposed his Moratorium and the United States stopped collecting war debts from its former associates, while these desisted from collecting reparations from the Reich. In theory, the American investors were now saved. But, in fact, they were not. On the contrary, in no long time many of the private debts as well as the war debts were covered by those moratoria which were destined to prove the preface to default. Evading all responsibility itself, the United States Government had permitted and even encouraged its citizens to send their money to Europe in the interests alike of world peace and of domestic prosperity. But the net result of the policy first outlined by Mr. Hughes at New Haven had been defaults upon the new loans without the arrival of assured peace.

By 1933, when Hitler came to power, it was, then, obvious that the European phase of American peace policy was bankrupt. The effort to prevent our right hand from knowing what our left was doing had resulted in getting both hands equally badly burned. But meantime the peril of war in Europe was mounting visibly, day by day and week by week. Simultaneously too, something was happening in Asia, for in the autumn of 1931, the Japanese stuck a bayonet right through the Covenant of the League, the Washington Treaties, and the Kellogg Pact.

Precisely at the same moment that Japanese cannon were thundering along the Shaho and Japanese troops fighting in the suburbs of Shanghai, the United States was, moreover, crossing the famous bridge between Geneva and Washington which the Kellogg Pact constituted. When, however, faithful to its promise to come to council, the United States had joined the rest of the world in protesting against Japanese aggression in China and thus invoked the sanction of world opinion, nothing happened except that the Japanese, while staying in Manchuria, withdrew from Geneva.

At the same moment, too, the Disarmament Conference broke down fatally and finally, because the nations which feared a German or Italian imitation of the Japanese example were unready to reduce their armaments save as the United States was prepared to increase its responsibilities. In vain Washington now promised to come to council in case of future aggressions in Europe in return for substantial armament cuts by continental states. For now the Manchurian episode had definitively established the market value of consultation. All to no avail, too, the President of the United States promised that in return for reductions his administration would waive American neutral rights, when these might interfere with the League action against a treaty-breaker.

Within the span of three brief but crowded years, then, the whole American policy in respect of peace had thus collapsed. The Washington Treaties, the Kellogg Pact, the Disarmament Conference were all dead. The war debts and many of the private debts were no longer to be counted as assets by any competent bank examiner. Meantime, German withdrawal from the League in October, 1933, the *Putsch* in Vienna in July, 1934, and Hitler's public repudiation of the armament clauses of the Treaty of Versailles in March, 1935, all served in turn to restore the pre-war situation in post-war Europe.

Last of all, too, in the face of the Asiatic and European crises there was heard on this side of the Atlantic a new demand for isolation. There was also a bewildered indignation which alike accompanied the default on the war debts, the invasion of Manchuria, the breakdown of the Disarmament Conference. Somehow, it seemed that wise and generous American efforts to promote world peace had all failed because of the blind and foolish reluctance of other countries to accept American light and leading.

In reality, however, what has happened is simply explained: the American people wanted a world peace profitable to themselves without paying for it. They wanted gain without responsibility. They rejected Mr. Wilson's program because it insured involvements and commitments. They wel-

comed with open arms the substitutes of Mr.
Hughes and his successors, the unofficial extension
of American loans to Europe, the anodyne prescriptions of the Kellogg Pact and of the Washington Treaties, the inexpensive device of European disarmament without American engagement.
All of these, however, represented in effect an
effort to get something for nothing.

With the arrival of the great depression, moreover, the nature of the problem of peace was
changing. As at all times in modern history, the
territories and the natural resources of the world
are divided unequally between the several great
powers. And the effect of the great depression
has been to drive the powers possessing the means
of economic self-sufficiency to monopolize their
own domestic markets. To do this, these more
fortunate nations are more and more rigorously
excluding the goods and the laborers of the less
fortunate countries. But these goods and laborers
constitute the sole means by which countries like
Germany and Italy can acquire abroad the raw materials and minerals necessary to run their own
factories and foundries.

Germany and Italy, therefore, find themselves
in a time of full peace living under conditions
usually produced only by blockade in war. They
cannot obtain the raw materials to meet their domestic needs because they cannot sell their own
products abroad. But the result is that their ma-

chines are running down, their factories are closing, their domestic labor is becoming unemployed. It is as if the water supply of a city were suddenly cut off by suburban towns, which had determined to use for their own purposes the sources of that supply, actually located within their own limits.

As a consequence, first Japan in Manchuria, then Germany in Austria and lastly, Italy in Ethiopia are seeking by violence to escape from the fatal restriction placed upon their national prosperity by their domestic poverty in raw materials and by foreign practices in tariffs and currency. Their choice, in the words of Mussolini, is between suffocation and expansion. And, while the United States, France, and Great Britain, follow their present policies inspired by the doctrines of economic nationalism, there is no peaceful solution for the problem thus posed.

During the century and a half of its national existence, the United States has extended its frontiers from the Atlantic to the Pacific by evicting the Indian and attacking Mexico, and it has also established communications by sea between its Atlantic and Pacific ports by seizing Panama. It has thus created a vast nation which within its ample limits holds the necessities of modern industrial life to an extent unequalled elsewhere. But more than half as many Germans and Japanese are in Europe and Asia respectively, crowded into areas smaller than Texas or California and utterly lacking in most of the resources of modern industrial life. Having, however, achieved this incredible extension of frontiers and accumulation of natural resources, the United States has recently undertaken by its so-called peace proposals to abolish the means by which it reached its own ends, which was war.

Were American peace proposals to be universally adopted, we should be assured permanent possession of our great estate without fear of future challenge. But, precisely in the same fashion, the Germans, the Japanese and the Italians would be condemned to tighten their belts, resign themselves to a declining standard of living and await the inevitable arrival of social upheaval insured by material misery. In one word, the real implications of American peace undertakings are disclosed in the fact that they were designed to throw down the ladder by which the people of the United States mounted to prosperity and thus to deny its use to others.

To accomplish this end, the United States— and Great Britain likewise—invented the convenient fiction that war is morally wicked and materially unprofitable, because, obviously enough, that is the present implication of conflict for both. But it was not unprofitable when England took South Africa or the United States seized California. It only became unprofitable when the law of diminishing returns began to operate. And that

only began to operate when we had realized the
material ambitions of our people completely. We,
therefore, offered Japan, Germany, and Italy partnership in a peace association in which we were
assured lasting prosperity and they were condemned to continuing poverty.

In addition, not only did we insist upon the
prerogatives of isolation, where responsibility for
preserving order was concerned, but also we demanded that we be permitted to retain for ourselves
all the profits of past wars, at the precise moment
in which we called upon our prospective partners,
who had been less forehanded in their plundering,
to renounce violence altogether. Literally, the performance of the United States in respect of world
peace has been on all fours with that of a man
who, having won all the money of his associates in
a poker game, invokes the law to prohibit future
gambling.

But why should war be prohibited in 1935 instead of in 1848, thus assuring to the United
States the permanent possession of its profits and
denying to other countries the possibility of gain
by the same method? Always the more fortunate
nations have been trying to persuade the less lucky
that war has become so destructive that anything
is more tolerable than a new conflict. After the
Napoleonic Wars, the victors of that era undertook to convince peoples which were subject to
alien domination and denied the right of national

unity that it was better to endure existing hardships than to risk the horrors of a new struggle.

Always, however, these attempts have failed because man has ever preferred to die fighting for what he conceives to be his rights rather than to live peacefully under conditions which he considers inequitable. A hundred years ago, the Greek, Belgian, Italian, Hungarian, Balkan, Polish and German peoples each in turn resorted to war rather than endure racial and political inequalities. Why, today, should anyone believe that peoples who find their economic circumstances intolerable will be too scared to fight? And obviously, as Japanese imperialism, German National Socialism and Italian Fascism have demonstrated, such peoples have already deliberately decided that peace under present conditions is certain to prove less tolerable than war.

In practice, because domestic politics forbade American administrations to assume foreign responsibilities for the maintenance of world peace or to modify the economic practices of the United States, the domestic peacemakers and politicians invented, and the people accepted, the fiction that the problem of peace is a question of morals. War is evil and peace good. To outlaw conflict legally and to condemn it morally is thus the simple and sufficient prescription for permanent peace. The mission of America, it was proclaimed, was to set an example, which was easy for a sated country

to set since it had already satisfied by violence
all its needs alike in territory and resources. Let
other countries renounce violence as we now have,
so the argument has run, and no police force will
be needed to administer the law and no courts
to interpret it.

To avoid facing the facts of a real world, the
United States thus invented an unreal universe.
In that make-believe world, too, it undertook to
follow the line of least resistance at all times. To
avoid paying any price for preserving peace, it pretended that peace was a state of mind and not
a state of fact. Therefore, it indignantly rejected
the suggestion that it should imperil its own tranquillity or modify its own economic or financial
practices to contribute to the establishment of
world peace.

Criticism of the manifest confusion and mani-
fold contradictions of American policy in respect
of world peace does not, however, constitute any
basis for the familiar claim that the course of
wisdom would have been to renounce isolation and
to join the League of Nations. For, by that course,
the United States could not usefully have served
the cause of peace, since it could thereby have
done nothing to remove the underlying causes of
strife. Always it was beyond its power to modify
the ethnic circumstances of Europe or to remove
the economic inequalities between the various countries of the world.

It could have joined hands with the victorious states of the World War in perpetuating the decisions of the Paris Peace Conference in Europe. But that would have involved it in the permanent task of restraining the German people within the framework of Versailles. It could have associated itself with the satisfied countries of the world in the attempt to make the League the instrument for the preserving of the *status quo* everywhere in the world. But that would have involved it in controversy with the Japanese over Manchuria, with the Italians over Ethiopia and with the Germans over Austria. And, when it did endeavor to persuade the League powers, and particularly Great Britain, to act vigorously in the Manchurian affair, its urgings fell upon deaf ears.

To have contributed to the prevention of war, it would have been necessary not merely to advocate the revision of political frontiers which European peoples found intolerable but also to champion the abolition of economic disparities which Japan, Germany and Italy not unreasonably deemed to be unendurable. For, since the United States, itself, possessed a disproportionate share of the natural resources of the earth and, in addition, insisted upon exploiting these exclusively for its own profit, to share in the creation of a real state of peace in the world, the American people would have had to consent to sacrifices as yet beyond the capacity of any country.

In reality, there was nothing which the United States could have done in the post-war years to prevent war in Europe or to promote peace in the world beyond itself refraining from aggression, and that it did. On the other hand, all its various attempts to combine political isolation with material and moral involvement were invariably futile and frequently foolish as well. The notion that any country can harvest the profits not merely of an enduring state of peace but even of a temporary truce, without sharing in the costs of keeping it, was patently absurd. But that was the assumption which underlay the Kellogg Pact, the Washington Treaties and the various American disarmament proposals.

As they sought to collect the war debts, while maintaining an export surplus and imposing a protective tariff, so the American people undertook to promote world peace while preserving the tradition of isolation and rejecting every form of foreign involvement. They talked impressively of substituting a reign of law for the sway of war but they steadily refused to join the World Court and firmly resisted every proposal to create a system of world police. But without courts to interpret and police to enforce it, what is the value of law, whether it be domestic or international?

When, moreover, all their proposals fell by the wayside, the American people turned to the construction of a navy " second to none," satisfied that

they had contributed their full share to the prevention of war and that their efforts had failed
only because of the blindness, folly and insincerity
of other peoples whose actual dangers they had
always ignored and whose pressing economic problems they had never even considered.

CHAPTER THREE

SECURITY

The World War not only left the United States
with an inheritance of economic and political issues which were new but also with a legacy of
naval problems which were novel. After, as before
the conflict, the American people still saw the
problem of national security almost exclusively in
naval terms. But what was novel was the post-
war insistence upon parity with Great Britain.
And, like the war debts, this question of naval
equality with the hitherto supreme seapower had
its origin in accident.

At the outset of his lectures at the *École de
Guerre,* Marshal Foch, acting as instructor for the
future generals of France, was accustomed to ask,
when a new campaign or battle was to be considered—" What was the objective? " What he
desired his pupils to grasp at once were the purposes in the minds of the opposing commanders.
Next in order came his interrogation as to the
means of opponents to carry out their respective
plans.

Obviously, the same questions must be faced in
considering the naval policy of any country. Nor
is it less evident that the answer to the second
question must be contingent upon that made to the

first. For a navy is not a mere collection of ships whose types and armaments have been left to hazard. On the contrary, a navy, like an army, is an instrument of national policy and everything about it must depend upon the nature of the policy it is to serve. All else will, moreover, depend upon whether that policy is offensive or defensive. Obviously, many other considerations will also exert influence, notably the distance between naval bases, the importance for national existence of imports from abroad, the extent of sea lanes which must be protected and a host of other details, which vary with the country; but all these are subordinate to the primary consideration.

Before 1914, the national policy of the United States was defensive and, in respect of Europe, its strategical situation was secure. Nominally, the mission of the fleet stationed in the Atlantic was to prevent invasion and to uphold the Monroe and Caribbean Doctrines; practically, that mission was imaginary because no threat of invasion or challenge of doctrine was discoverable beyond the Atlantic.

In fact, so far from contemplating any aggression in either of the Americas, Europe, after 1905, was consciously preparing at home for the great struggle already imminent. The challenge to British sea power, and, therefore, to British security, inherent in the German naval program had, moreover, led to a gradual concentration of the naval

6

forces of the three great maritime states, Britain, France and Germany, in European waters. Having nothing to fear from Europe, American statesmanship, therefore, properly paid no heed to the strength of the fleets of the European powers. The fact that the British, German and French fleets were superior to the American was disregarded. The notion that American security depended upon naval parity with England was never even seriously advanced.

In respect of the Pacific, however, the state of mind in the United States was otherwise. In the Spanish-American War, we had taken the Philippines. After the Russian defeat in the Manchurian War, there had gradually developed a suspicion on this side of the Pacific that the Japanese cherished an ambition to possess these islands and, little by little, American policy had fashioned its naval instrument with the purpose to insure our position in the Far East against a prospective Japanese challenge. Thus, in the battleline we had, even before the World War, undertaken to establish a supremacy of approximately 5-3, and that ratio, while, of course, it had no treaty standing, represented the judgment of American naval opinion as to what constituted a reasonable margin of safety.

As a practical matter, therefore, the American fleet was constructed almost exclusively with the idea of holding the Philippines against Japan although in American calculations the doctrine of the Open Door in China was by no means wholly ignored. And that purpose not only explained the ratio of strength but also the type of ship. For the distance between Manila and San Francisco made necessary large ships, which alone would possess the requisite steaming radius.

The outbreak of the World War, however, raising as it did almost instantaneously the question of the freedom of the seas and the problem of defending neutral rights, produced a profound change in American public opinion. Naturally, if illogically, a strong fleet came to seem the single means alike of defending our rights and of insuring our neutrality. That assumption was illogical, because against Britain and France the weapon of the embargo could always have been employed with deadly effect, while, since the seas were already closed to the Germans so far as trade and commerce were concerned, we could only uphold our maritime rights against them by joining their enemies in land operations.

Nevertheless, by 1916 the country had become convinced that a strong fleet alone could spell security for it and in that year there was undertaken a naval program deliberately designed to provide the United States with a fleet which, in the phrase then and thereafter familiar, should be " second to none." That new fleet, thus conceived and created, was, however, almost exclusively limited to capital ships, although when we entered the war, and thus shared in the solution of the submarine problem, a rapid expansion in destroyers also took place.

By 1921, when the Harding administration came to office, the situation was this: built and building, the United States had enough capital ships to insure it supremacy in the fighting line, although in cruisers it lagged far behind the British. In that same year, moreover, the German fleet was beneath the waters of Scapa Flow and the French had become insignificant because our associates of the war had been compelled to use their steel for shells and not for ships.

The British were now confronted by the fact that, unless they undertook to engage in a race in naval armaments with the United States, they would within two years have lost the trident which they had so long held. In the state of their post-war finances, they were not tempted to competition to recover a vanishing superiority. And to attain and maintain the supremacy already within its grasp, the United States would be called upon to incur vast and continuing expenses.

There was, moreover, manifestly no clash in policy between the two countries. Neither had any reason to expect attack by the other, both peoples were essentially defensive in spirit. As a consequence, sensible statesmen in both countries promptly began to look for an adjustment calculated to spare unnecessary expense and also to abolish a danger of distrust certain to accompany competition. Such was the foundation upon which was developed the first act in the post-war performance of American naval policy upon the international stage which was the Washington Naval Conference of 1921-1922.

In considering the history of that ill-omened conclave, it is necessary, first of all, to examine the policies of the several nations therein represented. For not only the United States and Great Britain, but Japan, France and Italy, as well, took part. The Italian rôle was without contemporary importance, but success for the Conference was always contingent upon fitting together the purposes of all four of the other naval powers.

Up to a point, British and American objectives were identical. Great Britain desired to escape inferiority in the battle line without paying the price of parity in new constructions. The United States desired to avoid the huge costs of completing and maintaining the fleet she was already building. In such a situation, moreover, the single basis of transaction was equality. For, although after the war there existed no reason of policy to warrant an American demand for parity with Britain, as there had been none before the conflict, America now had built and was building the capital ships required to insure superiority and accordingly the best bargain the British could hope for in the battleline was equality.

In the field of cruisers, where her superiority was still overwhelming, Britain could, to be sure, hope to do better. But only if her diplomacy were more skilful than the American, because, as a matter of horse-trading, it was unlikely that the United States would concede parity in the category in which it had prospective superiority, without claiming equality in another where its disadvantage was patent.

On the other hand, any agreement the British made was bound to be contingent upon her retention of a strength consonant with her two-power standard in Europe. For that, in the minds of her statesmen, was the traditional guarantee of British security. For the rest, the British and Americans were agreed in the termination of the Anglo-Japanese alliance, equally obnoxious to public opinion in the United States and in various of the British Dominions. But they both recognized that to persuade Japan to drop that alliance would require concessions. Finally, both were naturally resolved to restrict Japanese strength to limits which would constitute no threat to their several interests in the Far East.

But what of Japan? What was the objective of her national policy and what was the extent of the naval instrument she would insist upon possessing? In theory, Japanese policy, like British and American, was defensive and only upon that theory was negotiation possible at all. But what

Japan actually desired, although her ulterior purpose was not disclosed until long after, was an agreement that would, in effect, insure her tactical superiority in the waters that wash the Chinese coast, for already she was looking forward to that Manchurian Adventure which came a decade later.

To accomplish that objective, Japan, at the Washington Conference, consented to surrender the Anglo-Japanese Alliance and to accept a British-American-Japanese ratio of naval strength of 5-5-3, in return for a British agreement to renounce the right to extend the fortifications of Hong Kong and an American promise not to expand those of the Philippines, Alaska or Guam. Thus, in fact, the Japanese threw the British back upon Singapore and the Americans upon Hawaii as advanced naval bases and deprived both of the power to interfere with their Manchurian designs.

Nominally, to be sure, the Japanese tied their own hands by signing the famous Washington Treaty which pledged each of the signatory powers to respect the territorial rights of the others—and China was a signatory power—and to come to council in case any country broke its solemn pledge. In reality, however, at the price of a scrap of paper, Japan acquired for herself a free hand in her future dealings with China. And the United States, in effect, resigned the means to defend the Philippines, the possession of which had been a primary concern of national policy before 1914 and in addition, the consideration which had determined the size and character of the American navy.

There remained the French. Between 1919 and 1921 they had been engaged in a bitter struggle with the British over Germany. Their major objective, then as always, was to acquire a British guarantee of their own security against future German attack. So far they had failed to obtain it. To Washington, they came, therefore, uninterested in the naval issue itself, but ready to support the United States against Great Britain in the struggle they mistakenly imagined would be waged between the two English-speaking countries. For to their logical minds voluntary British assent to American naval parity was unthinkable. In the battle which they foresaw, they hoped to regain American favor and recapture American support for their European policy.

When, however, from the first day, Balfour and Hughes worked in complete harmony, French isolation was complete. But, although isolated, France was far from helpless, since she was, at the moment, engaged in the creation of a great submarine fleet. For the British, with the memories of 1917 barely five years off, the menace of the submarine was still real. To meet that challenge, they depended upon cruisers and, if France should decline to limit submarines, Britain perforce must refuse to limit cruisers. When, too, Mr. Hughes seemed to ignore the French and consort with the

British, French resentment dictated a French reprisal.

As a consequence, Mr. Hughes presently found himself faced by the choice between confessing that his conference was a failure and consenting to scrap American excess tonnage in capital ships without obtaining parity in cruisers. And this would be tantamount to resigning the only bargaining point he had with the British. But at this stage domestic political considerations entered into the situation. The Republican administration needed a successful conference to set against the still recent Democratic failure in Paris. The country was, moreover, unaware as yet of the technical aspects of the naval question. Accordingly, it could easily be persuaded to accept, as a gain for peace and a recognition of parity, an adjustment in capital ships. The conference, with its apparent settlement in the Asiatic detail and its partial progress in respect of Europe, could then be " sold " to the country as a " step " and, in fact, a long step toward peace. For the rest, responsibility for restriction of the results was already saddled upon the French.

In sum, then, the results of the Washington Conference were twofold. Japan acquired tactical supremacy in the Far East for her navy. Great Britain rid herself of the danger of sinking to second place in the battleline, without resigning her decisive superiority in cruisers. But thereafter it was no longer possible for the United States to defend the Philippines and it had not yet acquired parity with Great Britain in naval strength. Nor did it possess any further naval resources to bring either Japan or Britain to terms, since Hughes had consented to scrap the surplus tonnage in capital ships and to refrain from fortifying our naval bases in the Far East.

Failure to acquire parity, too, could not long be concealed. Thus, after a loud explosion of anger directed against the French, American public opinion settled down to a resentful conviction that British diplomacy had out-generaled American innocence, that Balfour had been as successful in out-manœuvering Hughes in Washington as Lloyd George had been in out-generaling Wilson at Paris. Now, however, the question of parity became a question alike of pride and prestige. Originally, the issue had arisen by accident, since public opinion was not alive to the implications of the war time naval construction program. At the close of the war, the reasons of policy dictating naval parity with Britain had vanished. After the Washington Conference, however, a sense of having been cheated inspired a demand for equality based upon mere sentiment.

The Coolidge Conference of 1927, which constituted the second act in the post-war international performance of the United States in the naval detail, resulted inevitably from the public opinion

created in the United States by the Washington
Conclave. To Geneva the Coolidge administration
sent its representatives to demand and achieve
parity with Britain. But now a new note had entered the discussion. The United States demanded
parity as a right, paid for in advance by the sacrifice in Washington of its lead in capital ships.
But it also demanded a parity assured by British
reduction in order to serve the interests of an administration, on the one hand, anxious to satisfy
the organized and vociferous peace sentiment of
the country and, on the other, to carry out the
economy program of the President.

The British Government of the hour, however,
was also subjected to a dual pressure. On the one
hand, it was bound to insist upon retaining a
cruiser strength consonant with the two-power
standard. On the other, it was faced by the conviction in Admiralty circles that the United States
would never spend the money requisite to establish parity and that, if British figures were set at
a sufficiently high level, British superiority would
endure. As a consequence, while the American
representatives clamored for parity at levels inconsistent with the two-power principle, British
stood fast for a strength irreconcilable with the
American program of reduction and economy.

Inevitably the result was dispute terminating in
deadlock. Japan from the sidelines followed the
struggle with intense satisfaction. France and

Italy ignored it altogether. Nominally collapsing over the question of the calibre of guns mounted on cruisers, the Coolidge Conference actually broke down because there was no basis for agreement between the Americans, who wanted parity cheaply, and the British, who were resolved to retain superiority at the cost of expansion. In the struggle, however, the position of both contestants had become completely unreal, for still no actual concern of policy divided them.

The third act in the naval drama flowed naturally from the second. Still further angered by what seemed the denial of a right already paid for in advance, the American government and people disclosed the fixed resolution to achieve parity by construction if necessary. In fine, the country was now ready to embark upon an enormous construction program, which must inevitably provide it with a newer and more powerful cruiser fleet than the British. And, since the financial resources of the United States far surpassed those of Great Britain, such a competition could have but one end.

The London Naval Conference of 1930, the third act in the naval drama, saw the settlement of the parity issue. In advance, Ramsay MacDonald crossed the Atlantic and conferred with Herbert Hoover. Sitting beside the Rapidan, anciently the dividing line between the armies of Grant and Lee, the British Prime Minister and the American President came to terms over a formula of parity

in all categories, which with minor emendations
was later accepted by the representatives of the
two countries in the English capital. But the
terms of the agreement abolished the last sem-
blance alike of economy and of disarmament, since
they imposed upon the United States the necessity
to spend approximately a billion dollars in attain-
ing the long-sought equality.

Once more, too, Anglo-American agreement encountered Japanese and French obstacles. Japan
insisted upon a ratio of 7-10 for cruisers instead of
the capital ship ratio of 3-5 of Washington and,
in addition, demanded parity in submarines,
patently a weapon calculated further to strengthen
her tactical control of the Far Eastern waters in
which alone she had immediate and vital interest.
As for the French, refused a British guarantee for
their Mediterranean security, they again declined
to limit their fleet. Perforce, therefore, the Americans had to agree to the " Escalator Clause " which
permitted the British to depart from the levels of
the London Agreements whenever the two-power
principle came into the question by reason of
French and Italian naval expansion.

The price of parity with Great Britain had thus
become a billion dollar construction program and
an acceptance of the principle that the size of the
American fleet should henceforth depend upon the
exigencies of Great Britain in Europe. Possession
of parity, however, bestowed upon the United

States no new security which had been lacking before the war, when the American fleet was outnumbered by the British by 2-1. And the size of the fleets of the two Latin countries, which was henceforth to decide that of the British and, therefore, automatically that of the American, as well, also was utterly without the slightest importance to the United States.

The fourth act in the naval drama was constituted by the decision of the Japanese at the naval conversations in London in the closing weeks of 1934 to demand parity with the two English-speaking countries and their consequent denunciation of the agreements alike of Washington and London. Before the Japanese acted, however, the full implications of the decisions of the Washington Conference had been disclosed in the seizure of Manchuria and in the subsequent failure of both British and American attempts to persuade Japan to renounce a course which constituted an evident and flagrant violation of the Washington Treaty, itself.

These attempts failed promptly and completely because Japanese policy envisaged possession of Manchuria and control of China as essential to Japanese security and prosperity. Thus appraising their interests, they were prepared to defend them by arms and neither the British nor the Americans were able single-handed to intervene effectively. Nor was combined action possible, because, as the Japanese had cleverly calculated, the troubled situation in Europe forbade British action elsewhere, even had England been ready to act with the United States, as she notoriously was not.

The effort of the American Secretary of State, Mr. Stimson, to establish a common front between Britain and the United States, however, provided the Japanese with the ultimate argument for parity. For the 5-5-3 ratio of Washington and London would obviously sink to 10-3 in the face of a combination of the Anglo-Saxon powers and even parity with each would not reproduce the measure of security which the old ratio had insured against England and America individually, were these nations to join forces. This Japanese demand for parity, moreover, constituted an admirable example of a conscious attempt to provide policy with the means necessary to make it effective.

Meantime, however, the United States had decided to withdraw from the Philippines. Thus while, in theory, Japanese denunciation of the ratios of Washington and London would permit the United States to expand its fortifications in the Philippines, in practice it was plain the United States would not spend millions and concentrate huge garrisons in a territory it was now committed to evacuate politically. Nor was it less evident that Japan could, if she chose, anticipate the United States in the effective occupation of Manila, thanks to her tactical superiority in the adjoining waters and to the superior military forces which she had always available.

As a practical matter, then, the United States was—and is—faced by the choice between recognizing the Japanese claim to parity and engaging with Japan in a race in construction and, of course, the British alternative is identical. Decision in this respect must, too, constitute the fifth act in the naval drama. In principle, also, pending definitive negotiations, the United States has rejected the Japanese claim and disclosed the determination to maintain the Washington ratio by competitive building.

But what consideration of national policy has dictated this decision? Would naval parity between the United States and Japan constitute any threat to American security? Patently not, for, on the same basis, American parity with Great Britain would constitute an even graver peril for England, in view of the smaller distances between the two countries. The ratio of Washington, like the relative strength fixed by the United States before 1914, was primarily the expression of a policy to retain the Philippines. The superiority thus maintained was a superiority designed to enable the American fleet to possess tactical equality in the Far East. Conversely, the Japanese could not hope to act effectively in American waters with a lesser advantage.

In reality, then, like the American demand for
parity with Britain, the refusal of the United States
to recognize Japanese right to equality has its
origin in a question of prestige and not of policy.
For, if the United States cherished any purpose to
employ its fleet to interfere with Japanese policy
in Manchuria and in China, generally, it would
require a far greater ratio of advantage than that of
the Washington Treaty. The fleet we need to defend the integrity of China and uphold the sanctity
of treaties is one thing and that necessary to insure
American security from Hawaii to Panama is something else.

To insist upon the possession of a fleet in excess
of the requirements of a defensive policy is, however, to establish in the Japanese minds the conviction that American policy envisages forcible intervention in regions in which Japan sees her interests
to be vital and is, therefore, resolved to fight to
maintain. Conversely, only upon the assumption
that Japanese attack upon the west coast of the
United States will some day be coordinated with
a threat by a European fleet on the east, can any
naval authority venture to suggest that Japanese
parity could compromise American security. And,
in practice that assumes an Anglo-Japanese alliance, plainly the most preposterous of all possible
mare's nests.

When at London the British insisted upon possession of a two-power standard in the presence

7

of Europe, they did it with a clear perception of the
bearing of the lessons of their past upon the problems of their present. But they did not insist upon
a two-power standard *vis-à-vis* the American and
Japanese because they realized fully that no combination of these countries was possible. In agreeing to American parity, too, the British perceived
that such equality would not permit us to intervene
to their harm in Europe and that no conceivable
naval superiority would permit them to defend
their American possessions against us.

The profound error of all American calculations
in the matter of naval power in the post-war years
has been the confusion of mathematical with tactical strength and the intermixture of questions of
prestige with considerations for security. To possess that tactical parity essential to defend the
Philippines, it was necessary for us to have a 5-3
mathematical ratio, in respect of the Japanese.
But obviously, on the same basis of calculation,
to fight in American waters the Japanese would
need not parity with us but the same ratio we required to fight with them in the Far East.

Political dispute with Japan over the question of
naval parity might serve British and Soviet Russian
interests, because it would distract Japanese attention and occupy Japanese statesmanship. But to
engage in such a quarrel would be of obvious
futility for the United States, unless Japanese
parity constituted a menace to American security

or the United States nourished any notion of intervening in Asia to challenge the Japanese policy in China. But, if we had any design, then the 5-3 ratio would be inadequate now we are surrendering our advanced base in the Philippines.

There remains one further consideration which has long bulked large in the minds of American naval experts: the relation between naval strength and foreign trade. For a full century, the eyes of the American admirals have been fixed upon the British fleet, as their minds have been haunted by memories of the War of 1812 and the circumstances which precipitated it. Seeing the vast expansion of British trade and commerce, they have reasoned that the British fleet constituted an important factor in the development of British trade and that the prestige incident to naval parity with England must prove a sound investment, insuring not merely moral satisfaction but also material profit.

Recent years have, however, disclosed the patent truth that the first requisite of foreign trade is domestic capacity and willingness to purchase foreign goods and that the possession by the United States of a supreme navy would not enable it to replace Great Britain in the markets of the world unless the American people were prepared to lower their tariffs as well as to raise their naval strength. For, while the presence in foreign ports of American warships might conceivably enhance

American prestige, the capacity of foreign countries to purchase American goods would still remain contingent upon the readiness of the American people to provide the necessary funds for such purchase by buying equally abroad.

That essential condition the British have always fulfilled and the Americans never. Nor is there anything in contemporary American public opinion and political practice to suggest that the possession of a so-called " treaty fleet," that is, of a navy equal to the British and possessing a 5-3 superiority over the Japanese, will produce a change in American economic policy. And, without such a change, the American Navy, no matter how formidable, cannot constitute a means of expanding American trade and commerce. As a consequence, its mission must continue defensive and the limit of its possibilities upon the basis of present conditions, will be the retention of tactical superiority in American waters. On such premise, moreover, parity with Britain and Japan constitutes absolute insurance alike in the Atlantic and in the Pacific.

CHAPTER FOUR

DISARMAMENT

During all of the years from 1921 to 1930, that
is, from the opening of the Washington Conference to the close of the London Conference, the
chief concern of American policy in the field of
armaments had been to reach an agreement with the
British and the Japanese on naval questions. Parity
with the former, the 5-3 ratio with the latter, and
agreement with both upon limitation alike in tonnage and armament were, moreover, actually attained at London but only after nearly a decade
of weary and acrimonious discussion. It was,
therefore, not until 1932 and with the convening
at Geneva of the great Disarmament Conference,
assembled under the auspices of the League, that
American views on the subject of land armaments
found full expression.

It was natural that American interest should
have been so largely absorbed in the question of
navies, because, as an agency of national security,
the American Army had, in peace time, played an
insignificant rôle. Nor had the war which had
changed so much else brought any lasting trans-
formation in this detail. Beyond the modest task
of supplying garrisons for overseas possessions

and for the coast defenses of continental territories, the army had no immediate mission. Some progress had been made after the war in applying to the American General Staff lessons which had been learned by association with similar organizations abroad. In addition, the Army War College, like that of the Navy, had accomplished a great deal in preparing officers to solve the larger problems of strategy and tactics.

Nevertheless, so far as the country thought of the army at all, it thought of it in connection with wars waged outside of national frontiers and not in terms of the defense of American soil. That was inevitable alike because of the comparative weakness of both the Canadian and Mexican military forces and by reason of the further fact that for more than a century all of the conflicts in which the United States had engaged with other countries had been fought on foreign territory. In the Mexican, Spanish and World Wars, too, it had been necessary to create a new military force and, as a consequence, the American people hardly thought of their inconsiderable regular army in terms of war at all.

The difference between European and American conception in this respect was impressive, alike before and after the World War. For the peace time forces of every considerable country on the Continent were organized in the light of impending conflict and designed to perform certain clearly defined missions once war was declared. Thus, for example, since as a result of the Franco-Russian alliance, Germany in the pre-war era was obliged to reckon with the probability of war on two fronts, her military forces had been prepared in advance to execute the famous Schlieffen Plan, calculated to crush France and take Paris before Russia could become dangerous.

In 1914, had the Italians remained faithful to their alliance with Germany and Austria, France would also have had to guard against a twofold attack at the Vosges and the Alps. In the same fashion, the British Expeditionary Force had long been prepared to act on the Continent and at the declaration of war was moved swiftly and efficiently to that portion of the western front already agreed upon as its sector. Russian and Austrian armies had been similarly prepared and the movement of European armies during the first weeks which followed the several declarations of war and the mobilization of the various national forces was actually no more than the performance of a drama which had already been frequently rehearsed. In all European countries, too, every able-bodied man of military age knew on what day, following the proclamation of mobilization, he must start and the destination to which he must travel.

Save in the case of Germany and her war time associates which, like herself were compelled by the peace treaties to limit their armies to insignificant proportions, all countries on the European Continent retained their pre-war system in the post-war period. In the earlier era, however, this European system attracted little attention on this side of the Atlantic and was at no time a concern of American policy. Confident that European armies would not be employed against the United States, the American people gave them little heed and their size was never in the minds of Congress, when annual appropriations were made to support the American military establishment.

After the World War, however, the standing armies of Europe did bulk large in the American mind, but not even then as a direct menace to American domestic security. Having recently been involved in a European War, however, it was natural for the people of the United States, to whom that war had brought only misfortune, to cast about to discover ways and means to prevent a future involvement on the terms of former entanglement. And to prevent future wars seemed the easiest way. Quite simply, too, Americans discovered in the huge standing armies of pre-war Europe one of the major causes of the last great struggle and saw in their persistence after 1918 an enduring threat to European peace. Disarmament, therefore, became increasingly an American prescription for preventing war.

In this American state of mind, there was a colossal paradox disclosed in the contrasting atti-

tudes toward naval and military armaments. As
to the former, the United States consistently and,
in the end, successfully, claimed for itself a navy
second to none, despite the fact that to make good
this claim involved an enormous change both relatively and absolutely from the pre-war situation.
By contrast, American proposals without exception
sought to promote the reduction of European armies to something like the dimensions of the American, although none of these armies constituted a
threat of American security. American proposals,
moreover, at all times ignored the political and
strategic reasons, which were responsible for the
size and character of European armies.

The fact that the Canadian frontier had long
been not only unfortified but also unguarded by
covering troops without having invited invasion
was cited as proof that disarmament meant peace
by those who ignored the equally obvious fact that
the Franco-Spanish frontier although similarly
destitute of fortifications and military guards yet
had remained inviolate for a century. Nor was
emphasis laid on the fact that the absence of a
strong standing army had not prevented the United
States from invading the territories of at least
three countries within little more than two
generations.

To ask France and her allies to reduce their con-
script armies was in fact, if not by design, assailing
what in the eyes of the French people and their

associates was the foundation of national security. Politically, France, from the March on Rome to the *Putsch* in Vienna, that is from 1922 to 1934, was always confronted by the possibility of a combination between the Italians and the Germans. From a military standpoint, therefore, French security was conditioned upon the maintenance of her army at a strength at least equal to that of the combined forces of Germany and Italy. And the maximum for both was rigidly limited, for Germany by the restrictions of the Treaty of Versailles, and for Italy by the limitations imposed by her poverty.

If the United States, in the interests of world peace, were to demand that France reduce her army to the Italian level and presently further advocate the recognition of German right to parity with both—and it actually did both things—then there could be no question that, if Italy and Germany later made a common cause against France, the French situation would be imperilled. Inevitably, therefore, the French demanded that the United States share the risks inherent in its proposals. As the situation stood, France had a certain number of divisions and that number had been fixed on the basis of existing political dangers. Since it was beyond the power of the United States to abolish these political dangers, it was for America, so the French argued, to share the perils or to cease from the endeavor to force

France to subordinate her own security to American prescriptions for peace.

The American response to the French argument was an effort to translate the whole discussion from the political to the ethical plane. Such a course was easily explicable, because on any but moral grounds the French logic was irrefutable. It was, in fact, unanswerable as a matter of right or reason. On the one hand, if the United States were so visibly concerned with world peace, its duty was to contribute its share to insuring that peace. On the other hand, if disarmament were the panacea for peace, once it had been applied on American terms, then no risk would be run by underwriting French security either directly or through membership in the League of Nations. By contrast, the Americans proclaimed their program as a gospel of peace, and, therefore, saw their mission as that of conversion and not of compromising.

European publics were, however, always something less than fully convinced that the American passion for peace was inspired by pure idealism. On the contrary, they identified in it a concern for the American material stake in Europe, represented alike by war debts and by current trade, as well as by the fear of becoming involved in another conflict. In the paradox disclosed between American naval and disarmament programs, too, European

minds saw proof of a hypocrisy which if uncon-
scious was not less real.

In point of fact, the French Army was the instrument of policy of a country whose purposes
were as pacific as the American. Nor was the
military superiority over either of its two prospective assailants claimed by the French, disproportionate to the naval advantage over Japan,
demanded by the United States. When, moreover,
after the futile Coolidge Conference, British and
French statesmen agreed to common action in support of types of ships acceptable to both their
admiralties but disapproved of by the American
General Board, the outcry in the United States
was immediate and unrestrained. Yet both countries defended their project as intended to abolish
offensive types and serve the interests of peace
and economy.

In a word, the United States was resolved at
all times to be the master of its own fate when
the question of American security was at issue.
It insisted upon its right to decide the number
of ships it needed, the calibre of the guns mounted
upon these craft and the tonnage to be allotted
to the vessels of every category. And, in every
instance, American demands were in accordance
with the national view of national needs. In vain
the British urged the reduction of the size of battleships, the abolition of the submarine, the limitation of the calibre of guns mounted on cruisers

to six inches instead of eight. For, despite the fact that each of these proposals would have made for economy, which, next to peace, was the basis of American advocacy of disarmament, they were all rejected temporarily or permanently as irreconcilable with American requirements. It was this rigidity of the American course which one day led the representative of a European country to remark that for the people of the United States offensive weapons were weapons in any hands but their own.

Actually, however, there was in this phase of American public opinion no divergence from the attitude of the peoples of all nations. At Geneva the French, the British, the Italians and the Japanese each presented a program of reduction and limitation of military armaments which accorded with their own geographical circumstances and strategic conceptions and because these circumstances varied so widely, there was no possibility of reconciling the several proposals. Yet each national proposal did carry with it unmistakable possibilities alike in the direction of limitation and of economy. But it also assured the security of the country proffering it at the expense of that of other peoples.

What was unique about the American projects was that, since the American Army was without large importance for national security, the proposals of the United States bore no relation to the

realities of Continental Europe, where armies
were the first line of national defence. Since,
moreover, no conceivable reduction of European
forces could bring these down to the level of the
customary military establishment of the United
States, they could be put into effect abroad without disturbing the *status quo* on this side of the
Atlantic. In fact, therefore, as long as military
disarmament was not accompanied by political involvement, so long the United States could urge
its proposals without cost to itself.

Of course the great mass of the American people were totally unaware of this aspect of their
activities for disarmament. On the contrary, although Wilson had been defeated, his influence
still lingered in many quarters and, far and wide
in the United States, people still believed that the
United States was a nation set apart, that its im-
munities due to geographical circumstances were,
in fact, the result of its peaceful policies. They
conceived that America had a mission in the world
and that mission was to bring peace and prosperity
to a torn and shattered Europe, by prevailing upon
the peoples of that Continent to imitate American
practice in the military department of its national
policy.

Remote from the controversies of Europe, im-
mune from the evils of a continent crowded with
rival and intermingled races, free from the continuing traditions of conflict, it was the mission of

the American people to bring peace and order to mankind by persuading it to adopt American ways. That had been the Wilsonian conception. But, at the Paris Peace Conference the American President had promptly discovered that European peoples could not be brought to accept American principles unless the United States were prepared to back these principles by guarantees consonant with Europe's estimate of its own needs. The Covenant of the League of Nations, therefore, constituted a compromise between the conceptions of the Old World and the New.

The fact that Wilson had agreed to such a compromise, however, although only by that means could he have achieved his major end, which was the creation of the League, led to the rejection of his Paris agreements, first by the United States Senate and later by the majority of the American people at the election of 1920. By those of his fellow countrymen who saw Wilson's original project as a moral and not a political prescription, his compromises seemed a betrayal of the true faith. By his opponents, whose chief concern was for national security and not for international peace, these Paris concessions seemed little short of treason to the United States. But, different as were the points of view of these two groups, their reactions to the course of Wilson at the Paris Conference were identical.

By contrast, the statesmen of all European countries and the public opinion and the press as well,
always perceived that the price of international
agreement was compromise. Thus while diplomats were often if not invariably denounced by
their fellow-countrymen for making bad bargains
abroad, they were not criticized for consenting to
bargain, for that was recognized to be inevitable.
This point was admirably illustrated by the procedure of the British after the French occupation
of the Ruhr. Alike because French stay on German
soil constituted to the minds of the English a
menace to their commercial interests and because
it also appeared a peril to European peace, the
British were eager to promote evacuation, but, to
achieve that end, they were forced to bestow upon
French security the guarantees implicit in the Pacts
of Locarno.

When, however, at the London Naval Conference, the American representatives sought to obtain a Five Power Treaty, fixing the future strength
of the navies of all of the maritime powers, they
were faced by the fact that, to obtain such a treaty,
embodying the tonnage figures already agreed to
by Hoover and MacDonald at the Rapidan, they
would be compelled to accept an obligation to
come to council in case of future crisis in the
Mediterranean. For the Rapidan figures would
insure Italian parity with France and accordingly
the French demanded of the British a Mediter-

ranean Locarno to preserve their present security. This the British declined to give unless the Americans in turn agreed to a consultative pact. Such a pact, however, appeared in the eyes of Hoover and of the Senate to constitute an involvement in European affairs, as it also promised to prove politically dangerous at home. Accordingly, the project was abandoned and the Escalator Clause was substituted for the Consultative Pact since no Five Power Treaty could be made.

Actually, in the relations between nations as between individuals, when one party in interest undertakes to persuade another to modify practices which although lawful are detrimental to it, the latter has every right to demand compensation, if it consents to change its ways. And that right is further fortified when the change proposed involves risks. It is only the reformer and the preacher who can call for change without proposing compensation because, in theory at least, adequate recompense awaits the sinner who puts away evil and turns to righteousness, since virtue is its own reward. The difficulty in extending this conception to international relations, however, lies in the fact that national evangelists unhappily preach only national doctrines to the peoples whom they are seeking to convert. Thus foreign publics identify the missionaries not as preachers but as patriots and see their moral principles as inspired by material considerations.

8

It was this circumstance which explained the monotonous failure of all the various American proposals for disarmament presented with so much noise and fanfare at Geneva. At home, both Hoover and Roosevelt, subjected to the double pressure of aroused idealism, which demanded that the United States do something to promote world peace through disarmament, and of alarmed patriotism, resolved that the United States should sacrifice nothing of its traditional isolation to insure tranquillity in Europe. Thus Hoover's dramatic intervention in the summer of 1933, when he summoned the Disarmament Conference to declare for a one-third reduction in military and naval forces all round, was swiftly buried beneath an impressive offering of funeral flowers.

In point of fact, this Hoover proposal was a mathematical conception applied to a strategic problem. Since it could not have affected Germany, whose military forces had, by the Treaty of Versailles been brought down to an irreducible minimum, it must have altered the existing ratio between French and German forces to the disadvantage of the French. On the naval side, it was similarly unacceptable to the British because for them the limits already fixed for their fleet by the London Treaty represented the minimum strength consistent with a national security at all times dependent upon keeping the lines of communication between Britain and the rest of the Empire open.

Roosevelt's attempt to establish a distinction between offensive and defensive weapons was similarly futile. Actually, during the seven years of its existence, the Preparatory Commission had never been able to determine not merely where the difference between offensive and defensive weapons lay, but also what constituted an aggression. For the British, submarines were offensive weapons, for the Japanese, battleships, for the Americans, neither. On the military side, the Treaty of Versailles, together with her own financial advantages, permitted France to possess an overwhelming superiority in weapons which the Germans and Italians, since they were themselves unable to obtain these, pronounced to be offensive. But the French, who were innocent of any purpose to resort to aggression, held them to be purely defensive.

Always in the American minds there existed the conviction that there was some mysterious connection between the smallness of the American Army and the greatness of the American passion for peace. Yet the rest of the world placed a quite different interpretation upon the exiguity of the American military establishment. Thus when Major General A. W. Greely, in conversation with Gambetta, told the French statesmen that the American Army of that day numbered but 25,000, the latter, with the memory of the still recent Franco-Prussian war in mind, remarked—" What good neighbors the United States must have! "

There was another aspect to the American attempt to promote European disarmament which was hardly less important than the consistent refusal to reward reduction by guarantee. From time to time proposals were made in Washington, or perhaps more exactly, trial balloons were released, with the design of suggesting that although the United States would not undertake political responsibilities it might make pecuniary concessions in return for the acceptance of its disarmament programs. The effect of all such suggestions was, however, uniformly unfortunate.

For, in the first place, the European debtors did not recognize the moral validity of obligations whose legal basis they could not challenge. To them, these debts represented America's contribution to a common cause. The attempt to collect at all seemed ungenerous if not unjust. The effort to use the debts as a means of coercion to force nations whose security would be compromised by the reduction of their military establishments to comply with American demands, therefore, awakened widespread indignation.

Once more, the true aim of American policy was accepted to be the preservation and promotion of American foreign trade and commerce, which must suffer in case of a fresh European disturbance. To that end and not in the interests of peace, the United States seemed to be offering debt reductions to parallel military diminutions but such debt reductions could not counterbalance the decline in national security incident to the restriction of armies. And so all such intimations fell upon deaf ears.

For Europe, the question of armaments was a political and not a moral issue. If the United States desired to concern iself with that issue, for reasons of its own, the nature of which was differently interpreted upon opposite sides of the Atlantic, then it must face the political aspects of the question. In a word, it was the same old question of the economic problem over again. To play the rôle of the creditor country, the United States had to make over its economic policy and, in the same fashion, to play an international part, in disarmament discussions it had to modify its political practices. It was for the American people to make up their mind what they wanted to do, but in both instances the rules of the game were already fixed.

Effectively to promote disarmament in Europe, the United States had to join the League of Nations and subscribe to all the engagements of the Covenant. The alternative was to leave Europe to stew in its own juice and bear the future costs of international anarchy uncomplainingly. For this was the price of pursuing a policy which satisfied American public opinion as best conforming to American interests. Nor was there any discoverable basis for the assertion that either disarmament, itself, or the American projects for the reduction of European armaments, did actually constitute a certain guarantee of peace. After all, the entire crusade for peace by disarmament rested upon assumptions as yet unproven.

If, for reasons of domestic politics, American membership in the League was impossible but American public opinion still demanded of successive administrations that they advocate European disarmament, then, to the European mind at least, the duty of the United States was evident. Under such circumstances it was bound to give effect to its disarmament proposals by consenting to implement the Kellogg Pact. That could be done by promising to join with other nations not merely in council but in constraint of a law-breaking nation in the event of a future aggression, which must constitute a violation of the solemn pledge of the pact, to renounce war as an instrument of national policy. For only then would countries whose military forces were large but whose political dangers were also obvious, consent to reduction of forces.

If the United States refused to implement the Kellogg Pact—as, in fact, it did—then it had only one resource left by which to promote disarmament. It could follow the British example of the

Locarno Pact and bestow guarantees where it ex-
acted concessions. Actually it was French concern
for national security which constituted the chief
obstacle to disarmament in Continental Europe,
just as it had been French action in the Ruhr which
most hampered British plans for the material
recovery of Europe. If the United States wanted
to remove the French barrier, it had only to re-
vive the Treaty of Guarantee which Wilson had
given Clemenceau in return for the " Tiger's "
consent to waive demands for the permanent gar-
risoning of the left bank of the Rhine from Alsace
to the Dutch border. Or, if this course seemed
inexpedient or impossible, then some other contract having similar implications could be made.

What the United States could not do, however,
was either to persuade or to drive the French.
For French logic was as proof against American
sentiments as the French situation was impreg-
nable to American coercion. And, as the event
demonstrated, without French consent, nothing
could be accomplished in the way of European
disarmament. That is not to say that French policy
was wise, just as it is very far from asserting that
it would have been the course of wisdom for the
United States to comply with the French demands.
On the contrary, it is merely to emphasize the
fact that what the American people desired had a
price and to get it they had to pay that price.
What was always true, moreover, was that the

United States could not have it both ways; it could not disarm Europe and evade European involvements. But from Harding to Roosevelt inclusive, that is what successive administrations backed by the majority of the American people consistently sought to achieve.

In this respect, British policy differed from American only in degree. Like the United States, England, although it entered the League as America did not, was at no time prepared to underwrite the *status quo* throughout the world or even everywhere in Europe as a means of insuring peace. In this respect, the rejection of the Protocol of Geneva by Parliament was as significant as the defeat of the Treaty of Versailles by the Senate. But where their interests were visibly at stake, the British, not at once and willingly, but eventually and grudgingly, did accept responsibilities commensurate with these interests. Always at Geneva British representatives labored to water down the commitments of the Covenant, but at Locarno in 1925 and in London in 1935 the British did consent to pay for what they wanted and could get in no other way, although, at the later date, it is true, armament and not disarmament had become for the British Government the single available resource for insuring national security.

The collapse of the Disarmament Conference and the consequent arrival of a fresh race in armaments in Europe was accepted on this side of the

Atlantic as the confirmation of the accuracy of American assumptions in the past and also as proof of the justice of the American thesis that disarmament alone could insure peace. Yet the vast sums which the United States was expending to bring its navy up to the limits fixed at London were nowhere on this side of the Atlantic viewed as carrying any threat to peace. For, to the people of the United States, the conviction that their policy was pacific deprived the size of their armaments of any sinister implication.

The deeper truth underlying not merely the American but also the world experiments in disarmament was, however, that there is no possibility of reaching an international agreement in respect of the means by which nations pursue national policies until these policies themselves have been brought into accord. Thus the single positive and definitive achievement in the way of limitation, if not reduction of armaments, in the post-war period, the Anglo-American agreement in the matter of naval parity, was only possible because the great mass of the English-speaking peoples alike in the British Commonwealth and in the American Republic were fully aware of the fact that between their national policies there was no real collision in objectives and that equality in naval forces was, therefore, similarly satisfactory for both.

Much was made in the United States of the theory that fear was responsible for armaments, once Europe had, after 1933, begun its new race in arms. Less, however, was said of the fact that, viewed objectively, many of the fears that found expression in armaments were justified when viewed in the light of the Japanese performance in Manchuria, the German in Austria and the Italian in Ethiopia. For, precisely as long as countries pursue policies such as these three great nations have manifestly followed in recent times, armaments, however insufficient in themselves, must constitute the only means by which their neighbors can defend themselves against perils that are authentic.

But, for the purposes of the present study, it suffices to point out that all American efforts to promote disarmament in Europe were without effect, because those European peoples which were armed were also confronted by dangers which could not be blinked, whereas the American proposals ignored the dangers and sought exclusively to reduce the means by which these dangers could alone be surmounted. Not impossibly, failure would have attended American attempts in any event, and those who assert the contrary are without proof to justify their claims, but the fact that failure was the inevitable outcome of the course actually adopted is beyond challenge.

Chapter Five

FROM WILSON TO ROOSEVELT

Viewed in retrospect, the history of American foreign policy between 1921 and 1935, that is, from Wilson to Roosevelt, must inevitably appear an almost unrelieved record of frustration and failure. The effort to play the rôle of a creditor nation terminated in an explosion which shook the domestic economic structure of the United States to its foundation. The attempts to promote world peace ended in fiasco. Parity with Great Britain on the high seas was achieved, but only at the sacrifice of those accompanying objectives which were reduction and economy. Finally, the parallel endeavor to possess mathematical superiority over the Japanese Navy eventually left the United States face to face with the prospect of a new race in armaments.

Explanation of this well-nigh uniform tale of disappointment and disillusionment is usually discovered by the American people in the fact of the World War. Primarily it is to the consequences, alike material and moral, of that great struggle that they charge their own miseries and misfortunes. In the larger view, moreover, that explanation is not to be challenged, since, without the war the post-war experiences of the United States would also have been lacking. Whatever policy the United States had pursued after 1919, nothing could restore the lives lost or the treasure expended by the nation in the conflict.

Nevertheless, it is hardly to be questioned that no small part of the chaos and catastrophe of the post-war years resulted not from the war, itself, but from the confusion and contradictions of post-war policy. The impact of the conflict upon American thought and tradition was so violent as temporarily to produce a state of mind at once bewildered and bemuddled. And bewilderment was further intensified by the course pursued by Woodrow Wilson at the Paris Conference and the revolution in American policy which acceptance of his peace program would have produced.

This confusion of thought and policy which followed upon the close of the World War was not entirely without precedent in American history. On the contrary, it had happened once before, although on a much smaller scale and chiefly in the political field. Thus as a result of the Spanish-American War, the American people had seemed, for a brief moment at least, launched upon a course totally at variance with that which they had hitherto followed throughout their previous history. Precisely as, after 1918, internationalism promised to supplant traditional isolation, so after

1898, imperialism had appeared likely to take its place.

By the annexation of the Philippines, the United States had taken its stand among the colonial powers of the world and seemed about to embark upon an adventure which had recently been illustrated by the action of Cecil Rhodes and immortalized by the verse of Rudyard Kipling. In that remote and forgotten day, when imperialism was in the air, the American people were, moreover, stirred by an idealistic concern for the intellectual and material welfare of backward peoples as, twenty years later, they were similarly moved by responsibility for the peace of the world. Once more, too, moral fervor paralleled material interest in prospective profit.

Only those who were alive at the time can quite appreciate the intensity of the struggle between the imperialists and anti-imperialists in the first years of the present century. Yet in no long time tradition triumphed over innovation and, as a consequence, the United States returned to the habit of isolation and to the practice of protection. Thus, a generation after the conquest of the Philippines, the desire to escape conflict in the Orient and the demand of domestic sugar producers for defense against the competition of the Islands combined to dictate American recognition of the independence of the inhabitants of their single considerable colonial possession.

Looking backward now to the days which immediately succeeded the World War, it is hard to understand how there could have been any serious belief that the American people were more likely after 1918 than after the Spanish-American conflict to desert their old political idols and to pursue new and strange gods, this time international and not imperialistic. Nor is it less surprising that the precedent of 1918 was forgotten in the period which followed the European struggle. For in that precedent was embodied a clear forecast of what was to happen again twenty years later.

Actually, throughout the years from 1918 to 1935, there was no question in the minds of the majority of the American people as to what they wanted most. Never at any moment was there for them any doubt as to the wisdom of remaining faithful to the two principles of isolation and protection. Their difficulty arose from the fact that after 1921 political leaders whom they trusted continued to tell them that they could avoid European involvements and retain the monopoly of their domestic market and at the same time promote peace in Europe and play the part of a creditor country. And, believing that these things were possible, the American people were not only willing but eager to undertake the double rôle.

The United States of the first year of the Wilson administration had been completely self-contained politically and almost but not quite self-sufficient economically. By instinct and by experience it had become steadfast in the gospel of isolation taught by the Father of his Country, himself, and in the doctrine of protection enunciated by the last Republican President of the nineteenth century; Washington and McKinley were thus the symbols of American policy in the prewar era.

In the great electoral battle of 1920, the battlecry of the Republican Party had been " Back to Normalcy." Washington's prescription for national security and McKinley's prospectus of prosperity had thus been invoked with equal effectiveness against the party and candidate proclaiming Woodrow Wilson's new program of internationalism. Once this issue was raised, moreover, there was no permanent doubt in the minds of the American people as to what their decision must be. Thus they voted by an overwhelming majority to go back to " Normalcy " and thereby to return to the faith of Washington and McKinley.

But, economically, the United States of Warren G. Harding was almost as far removed from the America of William McKinley as it was politically from that of George Washington. Politically it had only recently been involved in precisely the kind of European conflict against which the first President had warned his fellow countrymen. In addition, the conflict, itself, had transformed the United States from a debtor nation to the extent of $2,000,000,000 to a creditor country to the tune of $14,000,000,000. Involvement in the World War had, moreover, established the fact that isolation was no sure guarantee against European entanglements, while the size of the new American stake in the Old World constituted a further reason for trying to prevent another war which not only might bring America in again but also must destroy its investment in Europe.

The Republican opponents of Woodrow Wilson and all of his works had, moreover, assured the American people that it was possible to restore the material profits of " Normalcy " and also to find a new way to accomplish what the Democratic President had undertaken to bring about by his League, namely, to prevent another war in Europe. And, in addition, they had pledged themselves to collect the war debts and to keep American exports at their contemporary high level. By implication they accepted the Wilsonian premise that European peace had now become a concern of American policy for material as well as for moral reasons. At the same time, however, they promised that, in promoting peace, preserving the existing export surplus and collecting the foreign debts, they would never deviate a hair's breadth from the true religion of isolation and protection.

Such a performance was, of course, beyond the powers alike of men and gods. But thenceforth the successive Republican Presidents were the

prisoners of their party's promises. To have remained truly faithful to the old flag, however,
the Republican administrations after 1920 must
have rid themselves of the new encumbrances.
Their single alternative was to haul down that
banner with its double device " Isolation and Protection " and to enlist under the Wilson colors
bearing the legend " Internationalism." Thus they
were condemned either to follow the example set
by the British in 1846, when they sacrificed their
traditional policy to their contemporary economic
circumstances, or to abandon the $14,000,000,000
of European investments which the war had
brought. But the first expedient was always unthinkable while the second had become equally
impossible by reason of the promises made in the
campaign of 1920.

The three Republican administrations of the
early post-war years were, therefore, condemned
to sustain the illusion that had been created during the period of attack upon the Wilsonian program. And since the Roosevelt administration,
in its turn, accepted the views of its immediate
predecessors alike in the matter of the war debts
and of world peace, its situation was identical.
The course thus adopted, moreover, inescapably
compelled endless resort first to evasion and
eventually to recrimination. The war, itself, was
saddled with responsibility for the difficulties of
the United States in the post-war era and the

9

" wicked foreigner " with the blame for the persistent failure of American statesmanship to find solutions for these problems.

From start to finish, American Presidents were, in this period, confronted by the dilemma raised by the refusal of the exposed and apprehensive peoples of Europe to accept American prescriptions for security, which rested exclusively on moral and not upon military sanctions, and the rejection by the American Senate of every proposal which envisaged American participation in any but moral sanctions in case of foreign crisis. That dilemma was perfectly illustrated by the empty pretense of the Kellogg Pact. But when the Japanese thrust a bayonet through that parchment it was useless longer to hope that those European peoples who foresaw for themselves the fate of the Chinese would continue to put their trust in paper pacts. If the United States was unwilling to implement the Kellogg Pact by solid assurances, European peoples were, thereafter, certain to stick to their guns and reject all American programs for disarmament backed solely by moral sanctions.

In the economic as in the political field, American administrations were similarly condemned to resort to evasion. For Congress would not permit and the people of the country would not sanction any proposal to open the domestic market to foreign goods and thus to collect the war debts by the sole means available. There was, then, nothing left to do but encourage the American investor to buy foreign securities and thus to enable the debtors to pay what they owed. Accordingly, beginning with the making of the Dawes Plan, this course was not only permitted but encouraged by successive administrations until the crash which had become ineluctable actually arrived in 1929.

The same inconsistency marked American policy in the naval field. After the World War, the United States was resolved to claim for itself a situation which it had never even dreamed of asking before 1914. Nor was there any reason for such a demand, based on considerations of national security which had been lacking before the great struggle. But the United States did not merely demand parity with Great Britain and a relative strength *vis-à-vis* Japan, expressed by a 5-3 ratio. On the contrary, it also endeavored to achieve these ends without disturbing the economy program of domestic administrations.

Neither the British nor the Japanese were, however, ready at any moment during the post-war years to reduce their cruiser strength to levels which would permit the United States cheaply to acquire parity with the former or the 5-3 ratio with the latter. For, while American calculations ignored all other considerations save the size of the fleets of Britain and Japan, these two countries were condemned to reckon with other maritime powers beside America and also to solve a problem of communications which had no American parallel.

Always American proposals were consonant with American interests, but invariably they appeared in American eyes the expression of the idealism of the people of the United States. Europeans, however, saw the thing a little differently. They interpreted the attempt to promote peace abroad as a design to protect American investments in the Old World. Accordingly they identified the American refusal to accept all responsibility for peace as the disclosure of a deliberate scheme to get something for nothing. And the Japanese, for their part, were never able to comprehend why the claim of the United States for parity with Great Britain was in accord with eternal right and justice, while their own similar demand for a fleet equal to the American, was a final evidence of indefensible imperialism.

The Hoover Moratorium, in its turn, in American eyes instantly took on the aspect of a generous effort to save the world from an impending financial catastrophe. The world, however, viewed it as a last, desperate effort to save American investments in Germany from the effects of the economic policy pursued by the United States throughout the post-war years. And the French, who had no investments to conserve in Germany but were deeply concerned in reparations payments, regarded it as a deliberate attempt to sacrifice the rights of the French taxpayer to the interests of the American investor.

Roosevelt's attempt to save the crumbling Disarmament Conference by his proffer to waive the traditional insistence of the United States upon its neutral rights, where such a waiver would aid the League of Nations in restraining an aggressor country, in return for substantial reduction in the military forces of the armed states of Europe, was similarly discounted. For European statesmen, warned by their experiences with Wilson, were fully aware that Roosevelt's pledge would not remain valid beyond the close of his term in office. Nor were there lacking contemporary signs that the United States Senate was as ready to repudiate Roosevelt's engagement in this respect, as they had been to discard Wilson's guarantee of French security at the Rhine.

Japanese action in Manchuria, the Hoover Moratorium, the collapse of the Disarmament Conference, the default of the war debts, the reappearance of the threat of war in Europe, these events disclosed the progressive bankruptcy of American foreign policy, politically, materially and morally. The Manchurian affair demonstrated that paper pacts, no matter how solemn the pledges they embody, do not yet constitute any substitute for force as a guarantee of national security. In the same fashion, the Japanese action proved that the sanction of world opinion is still without avail to

restrain a government and a people once these
have identified aggressive action as the single
prescription for national prosperity. And the collapse of the Disarmament Conference disclosed
the fact that Europe had correctly interpreted the
implication for itself that the events in Asia manifestly contained.

The Hoover Moratorium, followed by default
upon the war debts and the rapid disappearance
of private investments abroad through the same
process, concomitantly shattered the illusion that
the United States could realize upon its foreign
holdings, governmental and otherwise, while clinging to the tradition of protection. Since the effort
to combine the rôles of creditor and debtor countries had always been absurd, in the end the truth
had to be faced. Finally, parity with Great Britain
had to be paid for by the sacrifice of the program
of budgetary economy and, henceforth the 5-3 ratio
with Japan can be preserved only at the price of a
race in construction.

For all practical purposes, therefore, the foreign
policy of the United States in the post-war years,
in so far as that policy undertook to combine isolation with internationalism and the rôle of a debtor
with that of a creditor, has, in the familiar Russian phrase, been " liquidated." It is true that
although the war debts are dead beyond denial
a remnant of the private investments still survives.
But even here, extinction is proceeding at top speed.

Thus, whereas in 1920 the excess of American investments abroad over foreign holdings in this country amounted to $4,000,000,000, measured in the pre-devaluation dollar, in April, 1935, these totalled but $6,000,000,000 in the 59 cent dollar, which was equivalent to but $3,400,000,000 on the basis of the older standard. No inconsiderable portion of the surviving debts was also in default and the market value of the remainder had shrunk impressively.

The stages of the journey are, therefore, easily identified. The United States was a debtor nation to the extent of $3,000,000,000 in 1914. It was a creditor country to the total of $14,000,000,000 in 1920 and of $21,000,000,000 in 1930. By 1935 it was, at most, a creditor state to the amount of $2,000,000,000. In the latest year, too, it was no longer pyramiding the interest annually due from abroad by fresh investments as it had done between 1920 and 1930. On the contrary, the sums due for interest and repurchase which were actually paid, were paid in gold and not in paper. But that gold was as sterile as the old paper securities had ultimately proved to be so long as the United States continued to support an export surplus, as it still did.

Would the situation have been better, both in respect of world peace and of American prosperity, if the United States had renounced its traditional doctrines of isolation and protection after the

World War and adventured upon a policy of internationalism and free trade? At the very least
there is nothing to be discovered in the evidence
in the case to warrant any such assumption.

Thus the greater dangers to world peace today
do not arise from issues which could have been
exorcised or from problems which might have been
solved had the United States accepted instead of
rejected the program of Woodrow Wilson and
thus have become a partner in the Geneva experiment. For the nations whose purposes constitute
a threat of war are countries which have frankly
renounced the principles upon which the American President undertook to found his League of
Nations, the principles of democracy and world
peace. Japan, Italy and Germany are training their
youth for war because they deem their material
circumstances intolerable and, in war, identify their
only means of escape.

As a consequence, were the United States today
a member of the League, it could only stand aside
altogether or associate itself with those sated countries whose material interests dictate their present
effort to preserve the *status quo*. Thus the choice
of America would be between joining Britain,
France and the Soviet Union among the great
powers in employing force to restrain Japanese
aggression in Manchuria, Italian in Ethiopia and
German in Austria and frankly abandoning the

principles which alone could explain its presence in Geneva.

In view of the present magnitude of unemployment in the United States, is it probable that conditions would be more attractive today if the United States had opened its domestic markets to foreign goods in order to collect the $14,000,000,-000 of foreign debts which existed in 1920? For, since the bulk of these debts was due from nations which are our competitors industrially, payment in kind would have had to be accepted in goods normally supplied by American Industry and, while the foreign laborer worked, the domestic must have stood idle. Again, for the Italian debtor, labor constituted the chief commodity in which payment could have been made. But would the removal of the immigration barriers have proved more advantageous to the United States than the elimination of the tariff walls?

Is it not plain, on the contrary, that the failure of American Policy in the post-war years was due, not to the employment of wrong methods to attain possible ends, but to the pursuit of goals which were themselves unattainable? The United States could not have established permanent peace in Europe even if it had abandoned its traditional policy of isolation. Nor could it have insured American prosperity by deserting the practice of protection. The blunder and the folly, however, lay in the attempt to achieve the impossible, while remaining within the limits of a national policy which was consistent with national circumstances.

It was that attempt which made it inevitable that the United States, after years of futile endeavor, should find itself in the situation which it occupies today. Nevertheless, for the mass of the American people what has actually occurred is as inexplicable as the eclipse of the sun to African tribesmen. And, like the latter, they can only account for the phenomenon due to natural causes by attributing it to magic and resorting to the pursuit of witches, foreign or domestic.

As a consequence, responsibility for the shipwreck of American policy and the disappearance of American assets abroad is placed upon the shoulders of European statesmen and international bankers. International conferences have come to be regarded in the United States as gatherings in which American innocence abroad invariably falls an easy prey to European guile and our well-meaning morons become the certain victims of the Machiavellis of a selfish but sophisticated Old World. Thus, after each international conclave, the American people again murmur the old refrain—" The United States never lost a war nor won a conference."

In point of fact, however, no explanation could fly wider of the mark. Granting that Henry L. Stimson is not a Talleyrand or Cordell Hull a Metternich, it is still possible to believe that neither

of these two great diplomats of an earlier age, had
his situation been the same, could have escaped
the failure of the American delegates to the London Naval and Economic Conference respectively.
In reality, American representatives to international conferences have not been, as legend asserts,
pygmies snatching at the knees of giants nor poor
but honest " boobs " fallen into a den of thieves.
On the contrary, without exception, they have been
public men of at least average ability, whose efforts
have been paralyzed by the political restraints imposed at home which have tied their hands abroad.

Invariably our delegates to international gatherings have met the representatives of other nations,
who were responsible alike for the security of their
own countries and for the fate of the ministries
in which they have belonged. These statesmen
have also been responsive to the sentiments and
public opinions of their fellow citizens, which, in
large part, they have shared. Necessarily each
delegation has had its own prescription of security,
which accorded with the strategic problems of its
own country. Precisely in the same manner, its
prospectus of world prosperity has harmonized
with the material circumstances of its nation.

Naturally, therefore, no foreign delegation
could return home, save to encounter personal con-
demnation and political exile, unless it were able
to demonstrate that the concessions which it had
made abroad were, at the very least, no more con-

siderable than those it had obtained from the representatives of other nations. Going abroad to bargain, European diplomats and statesmen have always to reckon with Parliaments and publics which will hold them to strict accountability for the character of the bargain they have made. They will be hailed if that bargain seems advantageous, tolerated if it appears fair, but damned and discarded if it appears a sacrifice without commensurate reward.

The American practice is totally different. By the people of the United States an international conference convened to deal with questions of peace or disarmament is viewed as an ethical and not as a political undertaking. For, if considerations of politics are to creep into the debate, then the American people are satisfied in advance that their representatives must stand aside, since in that direction lies the danger of involvement. The mission of our diplomats is to convert their colleagues to the excellence of the American program; their duty is to resist every foreign endeavor to persuade the United States to give concrete effect to its abstract principles.

Nor is the situation different in the economic field. On the contrary, when, at the London Conference of 1933, Mr. Roosevelt suddenly instructed the American delegation to abandon the advocacy of stabilization and admonished the representatives of other nations to drop this matter,

which was uppermost in their minds, because
stabilization seemed to conflict with the program
of his administration for recovery, applause rocked
the country from Maine to California. And the
fact that world confidence was shaken and currency
chaos perpetuated counted for nothing with an
American public, satisfied that for once, an international conference had not been accompanied
by any American concession.

By contrast, when at the London Naval Conference Mr. Stimson considered agreeing to a consultative pact, binding the United States to nothing more perilous than to come to council in case
of later trouble in the Mediterranean, American
public opinion was alarmed and Senate opposition
became vocal. Yet only on such terms would it
have been possible to make a Five Power Treaty,
since the French would not consent to abandon
their existing superiority over Italy unless Britain
subscribed to a Mediterranean Locarno. And
Britain, in its turn, was ready to bestow that
Locarno only if the United States consented to
make the consultative pact.

Always under such circumstances, American
public opinion assumes the right of the representatives of the United States to intervene in the
discussion of European political affairs as im-
prescriptible even when the security of other
countries is at stake. Invariably, however, the
attempt of the representatives of those nations,

whose very existence is thus called into question, to persuade American representatives to match concession by concession is denounced as the effort of the crafty diplomats of Europe to involve the United States in the disputes of the Old World.

In the very nature of things, however, the basis of international negotiations must be bargain and barter. No country can hope to impose its will upon others, where their vital interests are at stake, merely by insisting that it has discovered the single right solution of an international problem, a solution, moreover, which always imposes the expense and risk upon foreign countries while insuring to the United States a lion's share of the profits. Nor can the attempt to justify such a procedure by transferring the question from the material to the moral plane seem anything but transparent hypocrisy in the eyes of those called upon to pay for it.

Yet ever since the United States repudiated the compromises and concessions made by Woodrow Wilson at the Paris Conference in order to obtain acceptance for his League program, Presidents and their diplomatic representatives abroad have been constrained to adopt such a course lest a similar fate overtake their agreements. As a consequence, American delegations in international gatherings have always been caught between an adamant Senate and an exigent Europe. From the President they have received authority to hang their clothes on a hickory limb. By a watchful Senate they have been admonished not to go near the water. Under such circumstances how could the rôle of the United States seem to Europeans other than that of a "hitch-hiker" among the nations?

Obviously under such circumstances the decent and the common sense course must have been to stay at home. But that has never proved practicable, because each administration has been assailed from one quarter by the organized peace societies, demanding that America do its part to promote world peace and from another, by those whose concern for foreign trade or investments inspires them to ask American action to promote world agreement. Never, however, has this joint pressure of American idealism and American materialism sufficed to persuade Congress to break with its tradition of isolation or compromise with its fidelity to the principle of protection.

By contrast, the governments of other countries are faced by the double fact that the United States is too great and too important to be ignored, although at the same time they have equally to recognize that it is impossible to do business with it. The conviction that American representatives speak for an administration which may repudiate them over night, or be itself repudiated by the Senate with equal promptitude, is today universal abroad and explains the uniform failure of the proposals of our diplomats to obtain more than polite attention from international conferences. Thus during a single day American newspapers record the " sensation " created by such proposals but on the next they regretfully report that these projects have disappeared without leaving a trace behind them.

As a consequence, not only has American foreign policy itself failed because of its internal contradictions, but also the influence of the United States abroad has been gravely compromised by the performances of the past decade and a half. What the United States had attempted to do has ended in fiasco, the fashion in which it has undertaken to act has deprived it of the influence it might otherwise exert. And this is by no means the least serious of the consequences of American performance abroad in the post-war years.

CHAPTER SIX

THE FUTURE

American history in the post-war period has been
marked by two distinct but similarly violent attacks
upon traditional foreign policy. The first of these,
led by Woodrow Wilson, was designed to take the
United States into the League of Nations. The
second, originated by Herbert C. Hoover, when he
was Secretary of Commerce, was calculated to
establish it in the rôle of a creditor country. Had
Wilson's program been adopted, the result must
have been a complete break with the principle of
isolation. Had Hoover's efforts succeeded, they
must have insured a departure from the practice
of protection.

Once the American people had perceived the implications of these proposals, they rejected them.
Thus membership in the League was blocked by
the Senate in 1919 and decisively defeated in the
presidential election of the following year. In the
same fashion, the American people from the very
start refused to modify the tariff to permit an
import surplus and in 1929 ceased to make foreign
loans. Thereafter the experiment of Hoover collapsed as that of Wilson had failed a decade
earlier.

Despite the fact that the popular decision in each instance was emphatic and seemed definitive, the debate over both projects still continues. On the political side there are not lacking, even today, those who advocate the substitution of partnership in a so-called collective system for the customary American method of conducting international relations. And, in the same fashion, voices are still raised in favor of the expansion of exports without concern for the manner in which these are to be paid for.

Examined in the light of the events which have occurred since the war, what then is the right answer to the pending questions of American foreign policy? Should the United States remain faithful to the tradition of Washington and the technique of McKinley, to which it has now returned, or should it undertake new experiments with the ideas of Wilson and Hoover? In a word, what ought the foreign policy of the country to be in the future?

Before attempting to answer that question, it may be worth while to consider the nature of foreign policy itself. Actually the foreign policy of a country is no more than the system of strategy which it adopts for the conduct of its international relations. And the objectives of this strategy are national security and prosperity. Thus the real question to be answered is whether the old methods or the new constitute the better way to attain the ends which they both seek.

Patently, however, the foreign policy of every people must be shaped by two factors, the geographical position and the extent and character of the natural resources of their territory. In both respects, it is plain that states will differ widely. Nor is it less evident that while the geographical detail remains constant, the economic may vary as, for example, when a machine age replaces an agricultural era. Always, however, prosperity will be subordinated to security, because upon this factor turns the very existence of a nation.

The fashion in which geographical and material factors differ and the effect these differences have upon foreign policy is perfectly illustrated in the case of France and Great Britain. Since the French position is continental, it is exposed to invasion by land and, therefore, the army constitutes the first line of national defense. Again, because today, as frequently before in her long history, France is threatened with attack by a nation whose strength surpasses her own, she is compelled to seek security through alliances with countries which are exposed to the same threat.

As for the French navy, since invasion of the country by sea is totally unlikely, its mission is to insure the safe transfer of French troops from North and West Africa to the homeland in time of crisis. To perform that mission successfully, the French fleet must possess superiority over that of any prospective antagonist in the Mediterranean. Hence the insistence of France upon tactical superiority over Italy. Since the French do not reckon Great Britain as a prospective opponent, however, they are unconcerned over the fact that Britain rules the Middle Sea.

For Great Britain, by contrast, since its position is insular, the navy is the first line of defense and the mission of the army wholly subordinate. During long periods in her history, too, England has been able by reason of this insular position, to play the game of " splendid isolation." And these periods have coincided with the existence of a state of balance between rival continental states or groups of powers. Always, moreover, this policy of isolation, also described as that of " balance of power," has recommended itself to British statesmanship because it insures security without involving risk.

From time to time, however, there has arisen on the European Continent a ruler or a state whose ambitions and resources inspire and make possible an attempt to establish an hegemony. Then, because they see their own security at stake, the British have abandoned their isolation and allied themselves with the continental countries directly menaced by the existing threat. Thus, while from Canning to Salisbury, save for the brief interlude of the Crimean War, British policy was isolation-

ist, by contrast, when in 1905 the English detected
a German purpose to dominate the Continent and
to challenge British supremacy on the seas, as
well, they abandoned isolation and returned to the
technique of alliance, which Castlereagh had employed throughout the struggle with Napoleon.

Always, moreover, the British in recent cen-
turies have demanded and maintained a two-power
naval standard, thus insuring themselves against
any combination of the two leading maritime
states of the Continent against themselves. Such a
combination did, moreover, actually exist in the
Napoleonic era, when the fleets of France and
Spain were united, although only to meet common
destruction at Trafalgar. The two-power standard thus insures British dominance of European
waters and, in principle at least, guarantees the
population of the British Isles against the starva-
tion which must quickly follow the establishment
of a blockade cutting Britain off from the outside
world.

As for the British army, like the French navy,
its mission is secondary. It is organized primarily
not as a means of home defense, but as an
expeditionary force, designed to be used abroad
either to defend portions of the Empire or to
fight on the European Continent in the service of
the security of Great Britain, itself. Thus the
British military force has long been employed to
fix an enemy far from English shores and to act

offensively, even when British policy, itself, is
fundamentally defensive.

Now if one looks closely at French and British
policy, as each relates to national security, it must
become evident at once that France habitually,
and Great Britain occasionally, makes use of the
collective system to insure national safety instead
of relying exclusively upon their own national
forces. In both instances the collective system is
constituted by foreign alliances. Thus Wilson's
League of Nations was, at most, no more than an
extension of a European technique. His proposal differed from European practice, too, only
as the latter was limited and temporary, while his
was designed to be universal and permanent.

In practice, however, while both France and
Britain formally accepted the commitments of the
Covenant of the League of Nations, each interpreted them in such fashion as to reduce the new
collective system to the limits of the old. Thus
while the two countries were in principle pledged
to resist aggression everywhere, in reality the British watered their responsibilities down to the
Locarno Pacts, which bound them to defend the
status quo in the Rhineland, where their own
security was directly at stake. The French, since
theirs was a Continental state, were apprehensive
for their own safety, if war broke out anywhere
on the mainland of Europe. Accordingly they were
willing to underwrite the continental *status quo*

from the Rhine to the Vistula and from the Baltic
to the Ægean. Despite their solemn pledges given
when they ratified the Covenant, however, neither
the French nor the British were ready to take up
arms against Japan, in the Manchurian Affair.
For although Japanese action constituted an aggression as unmistakable as another German attack
upon Belgium or a " Nazi " invasion of Austria
could be, neither nation felt its own safety at stake
in the remote Asiatic province. By contrast, when
Mussolini contemplated an imperialistic adventure
at the headwaters of the Blue Nile, London's zeal
for collective action was impressive.

It is essential that this point should be clear in
all American minds, because otherwise the debate
over the relative merits of the isolationist and
collective methods of insuring national security
becomes unreal. Actually the French are unable,
because their geographical situation is continental,
to pursue an isolationist policy in Europe. But
where they can follow such a course, namely, in
northeastern Asia, they do. As for the British,
whenever they are able, they take advantage of
their insular position to remain in " splendid isolation." And membership in the League and adherence to the so-called collective system which
centers in Geneva have not modified the traditional
practice of either country. Thus the whole drive of
British policy since the war has been toward withdrawal from European commitments and France

has similarly striven to avoid Asiatic entanglements.

Therefore, British and French membership in the League of Nations constituted a continuation and not a change in foreign policy and the League, itself, became a convenient instrument of the national policies of the respective countries. No new risks were run and in another war, as in the recent conflict, both nations could hope that, thanks to the League, America would again make a common cause with them. For, having now attained the territorial limits and acquired the material resources consonant with national needs and aspirations, neither France nor Britain was itself likely to resort to aggression. And, under the provisions of the Covenant, all member states were bound to pool their resources to resist an unprovoked attack upon a League member.

But what of the United States? Its geographical position has permitted it to adopt the British technique of " splendid isolation " as a permanent practice. Unlike the French, the American people are confronted by no threat of invasion across their land frontiers too formidable to be faced alone. Nor can the rise of any ruler or state in Asia or in Europe threaten American security within its own region, so long as it maintains a navy second to none.

Thus while membership in the collective system of Geneva involved vast risks, it insured no addition to American security unless it were to be accepted as axiomatic that whenever there was a war in Europe the United States must be drawn into it. The only other practical reason to join the League was discoverable in the huge post-war stake of the United States in the Old World constituted by the war debts. But was it true that the United States must become a belligerent whenever European peoples came to blows? As for the war debts, was it possible to collect them anyhow? And the answer to the latter question was presently made.

It was true—and it remains true—that if the United States during another general war in Europe should undertake to exercise its right as a neutral to trade with all belligerents, supplying them with arms and ammunition as well as with foodstuffs and raw materials, then it would be likely to be drawn in again. It was just as true—and still is— that if the American Government should insist upon the right of its citizens not merely to trade but also to travel in the war zones, involvement would be likely if not inevitable. But, in the light of the still recent past, why was it to be assumed so lightly that the American people would follow the course adopted in 1914-1917?

Again as before, if Europe fought, the United States would have to decide whether to go in or get out of the way of the war. But could anyone mistake the evidence of past experience and fail to recognize the difference in costs between the two decisions? If America stayed out, she would inevitably have to suffer losses in lives and property. But how incomparably less considerable these were bound to be than the costs of war. And if the United States did resolve to keep out, what threat to its security could there be, whatever the nature or outcome of the European conflict? In 1914-1917 the World War had not come to America, on the contrary citizens of the United States had rushed incontinently to meet it in distant regions where it was actually in progress.

If the United States were ready to bear the losses incident to neutrality, losses in lives as well as in property, and to keep out of war abroad, what value for it could the guarantees of the collective system of Geneva have? Their value for France was evident, for the French could not hope to avoid involvement in a European conflict. Their use for the British was hardly less clear, for if the circumstances of 1914 returned, British involvement was almost as certain as French. But, as the record of the World War amply proved, American involvement was only sure if the United States adopted one of the two policies actually open to it, and it was under no conceivable constraint to do that.

Again, the assumption that American membership in the League could insure the prevention of war was an assumption and nothing more.

It was, in fact, an *ipse dixit* even more completely beyond proof than the assertion that the events of 1914 had demonstrated that the United States was forever after condemned to participate in every European conflict. What was alone susceptible of proof was that there was always certain to remain open to the United States a policy which would insure its belligerency.

If the case against departure from the tradition of isolation was impressive, the arguments against the abandonment of the practice of protection were not less formidable. In theory, because it had accumulated a foreign holding amounting to $14,000,000,000 during the World War, the United States was in a position after 1918 to play the rôle of a creditor country. But in practice, there was no way in which it could get its money back—or collect interest upon it annually—except by making domestic production pay the costs of foreign debt collection.

England could play the part of a creditor country, so could France, because both not only had large foreign investments abroad but were also dependent upon the outside world for most of the raw materials necessary to national industry—and Britain was obliged to import the larger part of its food as well. Neither the British nor the French workers or owners were thus called upon to pay the costs of realizing on foreign holdings.

Nor was the domestic investor in foreign securities faced by any problem in collecting his interest.

But the United States could not realize upon its foreign holdings either by taking payment in foreign goods or commodities. On the contrary, it possessed a larger measure of economic self-sufficiency than any other country on the planet. Its foreign trade consisted almost exclusively in exchanging commodities in which it had a surplus for those it lacked altogether, cotton and wheat and meat, for rubber and tin and coffee. Beyond that, it traded its own specialities, automobiles and farm machinery, for example, for luxury goods and wines. But an approximate balance between exports and imports could only be established because the United States accepted twice as much in services from foreign countries as it rendered them. And the major detail in this service item was tourist expenditures.

In a word, just as the geographical situation of France and Britain pushed them toward a collective system to insure their national security, while that of the United States dictated a policy of isolation, so the economic circumstances of the European nations made possible the rôle of a creditor country while those of America imposed a policy of economic self-sufficiency. American security could not be enhanced by membership in the League, it could only be compromised. American attempts to play the rôle of creditor country

could not increase domestic prosperity but only
lead to ultimate disaster, because there was no
way the United States could collect foreign debts
without suffering at home.

As the material factors in the situation became
clearer and clearer, the advocates of internationalism strove to prove that the United States had
a moral duty to perform, which was to join the
League in order to aid it in preventing war. That
was, however, to assume that there was something
the United States could do as a member of the
League that it could not do otherwise. But what
in fact could it do? Compel the German, Hungarian and Bulgarian peoples, who found the territorial decisions of the Paris settlement intolerable
to endure the *status quo?* Force the states which
had profited by these decisions to give back popu-
lations and provinces? Obviously either result
could be achieved only by coercion which could
mean war.

Again, was the United States, acting through
the League of Nations, to serve the cause of peace
in the world by defending a *status quo* which
Britain, France and pre-war Russia had established by war, thus opposing all efforts of the
German, Japanese and Italian peoples to employ
the same method to achieve the same end? That,
too, would involve risks and could lead to war.
But why was the United States morally concerned
as to who should hold the Polish Corridor and

whether or not Italy repeated in Ethiopia the French performance in Morocco? Why should American lives and property be hazarded to preserve for the French or the British the profits of past plunderings and simultaneously to prevent German and Italian acquisition of a similar booty?

Always it was urged by the champions of the League that other nations were doing their part to insure world peace whereas the United States was standing aside. But what were the other countries doing? In so far as world peace and their own security were identical, they were patently striving by the employment of League machinery to promote peace, but not otherwise. For them, Geneva was the seat of a political machine not an instrument to create and maintain a condition of equality between states either politically or materially. Yet, not until such a condition of equality was created, could there be discussion of peace. For the United States the questions of European peace and of its own security could only be identical, if it chose to make them so. Otherwise it had no material stake in European peace comparable to that of Britain or France.

If Britain and France had been ready to sacrifice blood and treasure to restrain Japanese aggression and thus give practical effect to the collective system, then, although British and French stakes in Asia are far greater than American, a refusal of the United States to share in the vindication of the sanctity of the Treaty of Washington and in the repulse of a patent aggression would have exposed it to the charge of evading the performance of a moral duty. But, in point of fact, in the Manchurian affair it was the United States which urged collective action and the League powers which hung back.

On the other hand, the attempt of the British and the French to obtain American guarantees for the *status quo* against a German attack in regions where their own security is at stake, was inspired by concern for safety and had nothing on earth to do with the collective system. In these premises, the United States, whether in the League or out of it, could not serve the cause of world peace. At most it could only side with France and Britain against Germany. Unless it be argued that world peace and British and French security are identical, the question of duty does not arise for the United States. But if that argument is pressed then the simpler way to perform our duty would be to make a direct alliance with these countries and thereby repeat the performance of 1917. But how could anyone argue that a new American crusade for world peace in Europe, necessarily conducted upon the same lines as the old, could be more successful?

Criticism of the current economic practices of the United States was also based upon things unknown and unpredictable. Thus it was often alleged that the present pursuit of economic self-sufficiency must end in a decline in the domestic standard of life. But not only was that assertion not susceptible of proof, but it was also just as reasonable to assert that the effort to expand American exports to former proportions and finance them either by foreign loans or by the revision of the domestic tariff would produce the same consequences as the similar experiments undertaken between 1920 and 1930.

Remedy for the most glaring faults in the present system of administering foreign trade was also asserted to lie in the transfer of the control of the tariff-making machinery from the hands of Congress to those of the State Department or of a new Foreign Trade Authority. But the trouble with such proposals lies in the fact that in the United States the tariff is primarily a sectional and political matter and not an economic issue, whereas, in Great Britain the representatives of various regions in the House of Commons frequently do not sit for constituencies in which they actually reside.

Were the United States to abolish its existing system and to adopt the British method or, for that matter, if it abandoned democracy for dictatorship, then it would be possible to fix tariff schedules and administer them in conformity with economic and not political considerations. Then it might be practicable, for example, to meet the clamor of New England textile interests for higher duties to resist Japanese competition, by the simple statement of fact that, since the Japanese buy from us twice as much as they sell, to raise our duties would insure reprisal and Japan would obviously have twice as large a target to aim at.

Actually on that day on which Congress marches in a body to the Capitol to abdicate in favor of a dictator, as the German Reichstag and the Italian Parliament have already done, it will still continue to assert its prerogative to control the tariff—until the gavel falls for the last time. And, pending such time, if a new Tariff Control Authority could be established, as it cannot be, it would need steps as broad as those of the National Monument in Rome to accommodate the members of Congress waiting to be heard in opposition to any project of tariff revision downward.

Today, moreover, the need of a president or of a political party for the electoral or congressional votes responsible to a particular sectional interest can and frequently does overbear counsels patently sound and wise in themselves. Politically the tariff is treated as if it were a traffic ordinance regulating the use of a one-way street. And it must continue to be so regarded precisely as long as those who fix its schedules see their reelection depending upon the fidelity with which they serve sectional interests.

No better illustration of this fact could be asked than that provided by the Hawley-Smoot Law.

11

For, if the United States meant to try to collect the war debts, this law was stark folly. Yet Congress passed it and the President signed it.

Today the New Deal, in its turn, is torn between the advocates of bilateral pacts and the champions of reciprocal agreements as means to promote foreign trade. But, since the former device makes no provisions for the admission of additional foreign goods to balance the expansion of domestic exports, its value must be *nil*. As to the latter, it is sound only if it promotes the exchange of goods not currently traded in and not otherwise.

What is usually overlooked is the fact that during the boom years the United States accepted foreign services in excess of those it rendered abroad to an annual amount of nearly $750,000,-000, mainly representing tourist expenditures and that these were the most important single item in balancing the export and import details. Thus between 1920 and 1930 the United States exported upwards of $56,000,000,000 in goods and commodities, whereas it imported but $46,000,000,-000. The $8,000,000,000 surplus in foreign services which it accepted thus went far to equalize the two totals. But, in addition Europe had to provide gold to the amount of $1,500,000,000 and the United States had to finance an actual export surplus of $500,000,000 by foreign loans. In the main, therefore, the export surplus in goods and

commodities in the boom years was financed not
by foreign loans but by American tourist spending
abroad.

Tourists and luxury expenditures, too, are beyond the ken of Congress, which watches with the
eyes of a hawk the imports of competitive goods
and commodities. Unfortunately, however, these
are possible on a grand scale only in times of
domestic prosperity and not in a period of depression. Therefore, it is to recovery that one
must look for a restoration of the volume of foreign trade rather than to foreign trade as the
means of insuring recovery. Stabilization and the
readjustment of tariff schedules which are un-
necessarily high will doubtless help materially.
But a sweeping downward revision of the tariff as
a whole is patently unlikely because in that direction lies ruin for the public men and party politicians whose fortunes are indissolubly linked with
the sectional interests of their various communities.

Accordingly, the political system of the United
States, like the extent and variety of its natural
resources, dictates a policy of economic self-
sufficiency. When, moreover, one considers the
tenacity with which the American people have
clung to that policy, although it has involved the
sacrifice of most of the $14,000,000,000 of for-
eign debts, accumulated during the conflict, and an
additional $7,000,000,000 in foreign loans, piled

up in the vain effort to collect these debts, the
likelihood of change now must seem slight.

Actually, the war did not modify the fundamental factors which dictated the character of pre-
war foreign policy. Nor did it permanently change
the American political parties. During the conflict and in order to win the war the American
people did lay aside their policy and their national
point of view. But because both were the result,
not of accident but of a century of experience,
when the emergency had passed and the war was
won, they returned to their accustomed practices
and to their familiar conceptions. That return was
due to instinct rather than to intellect, but, in the
judgment of the present writer, the decision thus
reached was sound, and destined to prove definitive, since he rejects the double assumption that
American security depends upon the perpetuation
of European peace and that, as a member of the
League, the United States could prevent European
conflict. Precisely in the same way, he holds un-
founded the further assumption that American
prosperity can be established upon a foundation
of foreign debts, either those created by the war
or those resulting from a post-war effort to create
an export surplus.

In sum, if future American foreign policy is to
conform to the geographical, material and political
circumstances of the United States, as it must do
if it is to be successful, then it will be based upon

the following prescriptions: For peace, arbitration; for security, naval parity; for prosperity, protective tariff; and for armaments, limitation. Implicit in such a program, too, must be application of the lessons of the war and post-war periods.

Thus arbitration must include within its sphere not merely the settlement of disagreements when the world is at peace but also of disputes arising from the invasion of American neutral rights when Europe is at war. This prescription for peace must also envisage consultation and conference with other countries but an uncompromising refusal to ratify any international agreement which envisages coercion whether exerted by military, economic, or moral sanctions.

Security, in its turn, since it is based upon the possession of equality with the navy of the strongest maritime power, must involve the recognition of the right of any other state to claim parity with the United States. Recognition of that right, too, cannot impair American safety, because mathematical parity will automatically bestow tactical superiority in home waters, which alone can concern the United States, as long as its purposes are pacific and its aims defensive.

As to protection, it is patent that both politically and practically, it is impossible for the United States to resort to free trade or to attempt to play the rôle of a creditor country. It is, therefore, bound to seek prosperity in economic self-sufficiency. Such a course, however, automatically restricts foreign trade to the limits of an exchange of non-competitive goods and services. Currency stabilization and tariff revision in conformity with the customary practices of the past can and doubtless will remove unnecessary barriers to foreign trade but the fact that the United States has a balanced economy must, in the future as in the past, dictate the nature of its policy in this field.

As to armaments, it is evident that the sole way to avoid costly and dangerous competition between nations is agreement to set limits to armies, navies and *matériel*. In this respect, too, Anglo-American naval agreement, expressed in the London Treaty of 1930, constitutes at once a model and also the only example of successful adjustment in the post-war era. Similar adjustments in the future, however, can only be reached under the same conditions, that is when there are no political obstacles to agreement.

Since, too, political obstacles notoriously persist in Europe, American efforts to promote limitation and reduction of European armies, must evoke demands for compensating political engagements, totally inconsistent with American tradition and interest. Thus while the United States can and should share in all attempts to eliminate types of weapons and forms of combat which all peoples regard as inhuman, it should avoid all participation in discussions of the size of European armies, both relative and absolute, for these have no direct concern for it and must involve it in European political disputes.

As to the Far East, since the American people are utterly unwilling to go to war either to uphold the Doctrine of the Open Door or to preserve the Washington Treaties, the government should abandon all pretense to interfere by words. Japan is in Manchuria to stay. Great Britain and France, with far greater material interests in Asia than the United States, have tacitly accepted the *fait accompli,* thus re-establishing friendly relations with Japan. We should follow their example, frankly renouncing the Hoover-Stimson policy which was at once provocative and without practical effect.

Meagre such a program must seem to those who still cling to the idea of world peace established by authority alike vested in a superstate and assured by a collective system. But, in fact, not only does it comprehend all that the American people are today willing to do but it also represents all that any other people can or will do at the present hour.

INDEX

Ægean sea, 139.
Alaska, 75.
Alexander I, 139.
Algeçiras Conference, 45.
Allies, 31, 32, 35.
Amur, 54.
Anglo-Japanese alliance, 74, 75, 85.
Anschluss, 8, 55.
Argentine, 34.
Army, *see* France, Great Britain, United States.
Asia, 9, 53, 56, 87, 139, 146.
Austria, 7-8, 12, 60, 65, 110, 124, 139.
Austro-German Tariff Union, 10.

Balance of power, 136.
Balfour, Arthur James, 76, 78.
Baltic sea, 139.
Belgium, 36, 139.
Bismarck, Prince, 14.
Briand, Aristide, 52.
Buenos Aires Agreement, 34.

California, 61.
Canning, George, 136.
Caribbean Doctrine, 69.
Castlereagh, Viscount, 137.
Chamberlain, Austin, 52.
China, 10, 42, 43, 57, 75, 82, 85, 87, 118.
Clemenceau, Georges, 107.
Coercion, 2, 7, 9, 10, 13, 16, 17, 19, 20, 48, 49, 104, 107, 124, 145.
Concert of Europe, 14.
Congress of Vienna, 13.
Coolidge, Calvin, 79.
Coolidge Conference, 78-80, 96.
Corn Laws, 26.
Covenant of the League of Nations, 42, 52, 53, 56-57, 99, 105, 108, 138, 140.
Crimean War, 136.

Dawes Plan, 51-52, 119.
Declaration of Independence, 14.
Disarmament, 4, 48, 54, 55, 59, 89-110, 118, 128.
Disarmament Conference, 8, 57, 58, 89, 102, 108-09, 121, 122.

Economic self-sufficiency, 28, 33, 144, 146, 151, 153-54.
England, *see* Great Britain.
Escalator Clause, 81, 101.
Ethiopia, 60, 65, 110, 124, 146.

Fascism, 18, 63.
Five Power Treaty, 100, 101, 129.
Foch, General, 68.
Fourteen Points, 7, 15.
France: army, 93-95, 96, 97, 102, 135 ; disarmament, 91, 93-95, 96, 100, 102, 107 ; economic policy, 26, 36, 120, 143, 144 ; League of Nations, 6, 7, 8, 10, 12, 138, 139-40, 142, 145, 146 ; naval policy, 70, 71, 73, 76-77, 79, 81, 129, 135-36 ; world peace, 48-49, 50, 51, 60, 124, 147.
Franco-Russian Alliance, 91.
Free trade, 26, 28, 33, 124, 153.
Freedom of the seas, 71.

Gambetta, Léon, 103.
Geneva, 2, 4, 5, 7, 8, 10, 12, 16, 19, 46, 47, 52, 57, 89, 97, 102, 125, 139, 140, 146.
Germany, 7-8, 8-9, 12, 16, 26, 31-32, 33, 35, 47-48, 50-51, 55, 57, 58, 59-61, 65, 69, 70, 76, 91, 94, 102, 103, 108, 110, 120, 124, 135, 136-38, 145, 146, 147.
Great Britain: army, 91, 97, 137-38 ; disarmament, 96-97, 100, 102, 103, 107, 108, 119-20 ; economic policy, 25-28, 33-34, 36, 143, 144, 148 ; League of Na-

157